Success with STEM

Success with STEM is an essential resource, packed with advice and ideas to support and enthuse all those involved in the planning and delivery of STEM (Science, Technology, Engineering and Maths) to school students. It offers guidance on current issues and priority areas to help you make informed judgements about your own practice and argue for further support for your subject in school. It explains current initiatives to enhance STEM teaching and offers a wide range of practical activities to support exciting teaching and learning in and beyond the classroom.

Illustrated with examples of successful projects in real schools, this friendly, inspiring book explores:

- innovative teaching ideas to make lessons buzz
- activities for successful practical work
- sourcing additional funding
- finding and making the most of the best resources
- STEM outside the classroom
- setting up and enhancing your own STEM club
- getting involved in STEM competitions, fairs and festivals
- promoting STEM careers and tackling stereotypes
- health, safety and legal issues
- examples of international projects
- a wide-ranging list of project and activity titles.

Enriched by the authors' extensive experience and work with schools, *Success with STEM* is a rich compendium for all those who want to develop outstanding lessons and infuse a life-long interest in STEM learning in their students. The advice and guidance will be invaluable for all teachers, subject leaders, trainee teachers and NQTs.

Sue Howarth is Senior Lecturer in Secondary Education (Science) at the University of Worcester. She teaches on a number of Science education courses and professional development courses.

Linda Scott is Senior Lecturer in Secondary Education/STEM Support Manager at the University of Worcester and teaches on the secondary Science PGCE course.

Success with STEM

Ideas for the classroom,
STEM clubs and beyond

Sue Howarth and
Linda Scott

Routledge
Taylor & Francis Group

LONDON AND NEW YORK

First published 2014
by Routledge
2 Park Square, Milton Park, Abingdon, Oxon OX14 4RN

and by Routledge
711 Third Avenue, New York, NY 10017

Routledge is an imprint of the Taylor & Francis Group, an informa business

British Library Cataloguing in Publication Data
A catalogue record for this book is available from the British Library

Library of Congress Cataloging in Publication Data
A catalog record for this book has been requested

ISBN: 978-0-415-82288-6 (hbk)
ISBN: 978-0-415-82289-3 (pbk)
ISBN: 978-1-315-88044-0 (ebk)

Typeset in Galliard
by Swales & Willis Ltd, Exeter, Devon

MIX
Paper from
responsible sources
FSC
www.fsc.org   FSC® C013056

Printed and bound in Great Britain by
TJ International Ltd, Padstow, Cornwall

Contents

Figures

Tables

Boxes

Acknowledgements

Many thanks to our colleagues at the University of Worcester for reading through chapters and providing positive and constructive feedback. We particularly wish to thank:

Anthony Barnett, Senior Lecturer in ICT, Design & Technology and Primary Science Education
Phil Collins, Senior Lecturer in Science Education, STEM team
Sue Dutson, Senior Lecturer in Primary Science and Design & Technology Education
Jane Moreton, Senior Lecturer in Mathematics Education, STEM team
Susan Wood-Griffiths, Senior Lecturer in Design & Technology Education, STEM team.

We also thank Jane Essex, Lecturer in Science Education, University of Keele, for providing many of the Science examples about cultural inclusion and celebrating diversity, used in Chapter 2, pages 28–29.

Also, grateful thanks to our families for putting up with us working long hours and for providing some feedback:

Kate Howarth
Andrew Scott
Alan Woollhead.

Introduction

What makes two extremely busy teacher educators come together to write a book about success with STEM? We have been professional colleagues in the Institute of Education at the University of Worcester in the UK since 2008 and during that time have collaborated on many projects that have cemented a shared passion for delivering vibrant and meaningful learning experiences.

In addition to our work in initial teacher education, we have many years of experience delivering professional development training for teachers both nationally and internationally, much of it focusing on enhancing and enriching students' formal and informal experiences of STEM. We have also contributed independently to a range of curriculum development initiatives and in 2010 began a productive period working together to write regular articles about running STEM clubs for *School Science Review* (SSR), the journal of the Association for Science Education aimed at educators of 11–19-year-olds.

Although already working collaboratively on a daily basis as teacher trainers, it was only during the early stages of co-authoring the 'Clubbers' Guide' articles for SSR that we discovered our shared voice for promoting curriculum enrichment activities. During meetings to select topics for the SSR articles, more and more personal recollections about opportunities seized and challenges overcome were shared and it became clear to us that we had 'more than enough to fill a book'. Hence the prospect of working together to write a book about successful practices in STEM education in schools was first mooted.

As well as being proponents of STEM enrichment activities for all learners, we believe in promoting opportunities that encourage a range of skill sets as well as broadening and deepening learners' knowledge and understanding of the STEM subjects. Variously referred to as 'skills for learning', 'learning and thinking skills' and even 'employability skills', the ability to work independently and as part of a team, to think through problems and challenges and to plan and prioritise steps to complete a task are essential complements to the subject-specific skills practised during STEM curriculum time. The encouragement of these broad skills underpins much of this book.

From the outset, we wanted to make sure that 'our book' was more than a useful compilation of hints and tips and series of instruction sheets for STEM club activities. Our work with trainee and serving teachers confirms that there is a huge demand for ideas and resources for all sorts of enrichment activities, so we have devoted a major portion of the book, Chapters 2–5, to ideas, help, suggestions, advice and rationale for successful STEM activities in lessons and beyond lessons, including using the school grounds, visits and STEM clubs. Most of the ideas are backed up with practical advice and alternative activities, so in a sense, these chapters can be regarded as a handbook for embedding STEM activities throughout the school and for giving pupils effective access to STEM ideas during their schooling.

No book about successful STEM practice would be complete without some attention to how to encourage more young people to value the contribution that the STEM subjects make to society. This also includes addressing the challenge of improving the recruitment of students into studying the STEM subjects after they stop being compulsory elements of the school or college curriculum. Chapter 6, therefore, examines ways of encouraging the take-up of the STEM subjects through embedding careers information and signposting into mainstream curriculum time as well as within extracurricular activities in ways that enliven lessons and reinforce learning.

Advice on health, safety and legal issues is given in Chapter 7. The legislative references in this chapter are primarily based on English law at the time of writing (spring, 2013), but as much of the chapter is about awareness of risk, it is relevant to all readers with the proviso about taking into account any additional national, regional or local restrictions on practice. The message we try to give here is that many more exciting activities and ventures are possible than is often believed.

Our background as educationalists steered us to include chapters to support teachers in developing the confidence to devise their own successful enrichment activities and Chapters 8–10 have been written with this in mind. Ideas are suggested about where to find funding and resources, including ideas from beyond the UK, and a taste is given of the many competitions and STEM fairs in which students and teachers can participate.

We included Chapter 1 to act as both a backdrop and a framework for the entire book as it sets out key political, social and educational reasons why the topics addressed throughout the other chapters are viewed as issues. The global economic demand for skills in STEM subjects has generated pressure on schools to meet targets; hopefully reading and using this book will help explain and alleviate such pressures.

Working from the adage that 'you can take a horse to water, but you cannot make it drink', we take the view that learners need to be inspired to continue with STEM subjects, not simply assured that they will be 'good for or useful to them'. All the chapters of the book are written from the premise that, only by giving learners insight into the phenomenal range of applications of STEM and providing them with genuine experiences of applying STEM skills, knowledge and understanding in satisfying learning situations, will they embrace one or more STEM subjects and wish to continue studying them – with success.

Even in the relatively short period since the term 'STEM agenda' was adopted in relation to educational objectives, the cutting edges of Science and Maths research and the capacity of Technology and Engineering to deliver larger, smaller, smarter, greener products and services have moved forward at a pace inconceivable just a few generations ago. We can only speculate about the range of factual knowledge and skills which today's young people will require during their early adult lives, but their dependence on STEM as citizens and consumers as well as through their participation in the economic workforce is certain.

Designing a well-matched education for young people requires a good understanding of the character of the challenges, so that appropriate processes and opportunities can be built into core and extracurricular provision.

By choosing the book title *Success with STEM* rather than the arguably punchier *Successful STEM*, we suggest that the contents of the book will not only provide readers with ideas and examples, but will also equip them with a deeper understanding of the STEM agenda so that they are able to make confident, strategic decisions about how to make lasting improve-ments to the STEM provision within their own establishments.

We know that our own professional development has been furthered through the process of researching and writing this book and we hope that our work proves to be the catalyst that starts readers off on their own journey of professional development towards fulfilling and successful careers as STEM specialists.

Websites referred to in the text can be found in Chapter 9.

Chapter 1

The impact of the STEM agenda in school

By the end of this chapter, you will understand the:

- academic, economic, political and social arguments behind the STEM agenda for schools
- evidence for current 'best-practice' models for successful STEM education.

What is STEM?

STEM is an acronym for Science, Technology, Engineering and Mathematics. It is used generically to identify circumstances or events that involve combinations of those subjects or individual subjects.

In educational contexts the term is often used as a convenient 'label' to refer to a subset of the curriculum or to define the character of extracurricular pursuits, for example 'STEM subjects' or 'STEM enrichment activities', as well as to describe staff roles, such as 'STEM coordinator'.

Beyond schools, the 'STEM agenda' is a complex concept linked closely to the supply and demand of STEM professionals in industry, research and academia. There is political and economic concern about the recruitment and retention of skilled staff in the STEM sector, as these specialists are responsible for a large proportion of the 'high-value' products required to sustain a strong, competitive economy. Factors originating in society and the employment marketplace, schools, further and higher education, and in industry itself continue to be examined to try to ascertain their impact on the supply of recruits with STEM experience and qualifications.

The 'STEM agenda', therefore, embraces the range of reports and subsequent targets and action plans drawn up and being implemented to meet the projected needs of industry and associated academia over the next decades.

STEM in schools

The National Curriculum varies across England, Northern Ireland, Scotland and Wales, but all students are required to study Mathematics and Science from entering school at around 5 years of age up to the age of 16, with some degree of choice in the nature of the course followed during the later years.

Other STEM subjects have a more variable curriculum presence.

- Design and Technology (D&T) is present in the curriculum for all students in the middle years of their education in the UK. D&T courses include:

- o   food
- o   textiles
- o   resistant materials.

Additionally, D&T courses provide access to computer-aided design and manufacture (CAD/CAM) and electronics and robotics. As D&T is not defined as a core curriculum subject in the way that Maths and Science are, there is variation in the options available and in the uptake of the subject.

- Engineering is not a requirement in the curriculum of UK schools and does not appear on many school timetables. This frequently results in students having little or no opportunity to appreciate the many facets of Engineering or the ways in which Science and Maths form some of the essential foundations for Engineering and its applications.

The practical skills, theories, rote learning and formulae practised in STEM classrooms, workshops and laboratories are most motivating for students when linked to real-life examples (Osborne and Collins 2000; Cleaves 2005; Barmby *et al.* 2008). There is also growing evidence (Ofsted 2011a) that the opportunity to work through an enquiry-based learning approach develops deeper understanding and increases the likelihood of continued study. The onus is, therefore, on teachers to interpret and illustrate topics using examples of development and application, linked to insights into how they are exploited by scientists, technologists, engineers and mathematicians in contemporary and futuristic contexts.

After Her Majesty's Inspectors (Ofsted) visited primary (5–11 years) schools in England between 2007 and 2010 to survey D&T, they strongly endorsed learning outside the classroom activities and opportunities for pupils to take part in STEM-related extracurricular activities:

> Enrichment activities were strongly represented in good curriculum provision. Visits and participation in local, regional and national competitions and initiatives provided stimulating contexts for D&T work. They contributed to pupils' enjoyment and achievement of D&T.

> After-school clubs were a feature in many effective schools, offering pupils the opportunity to further develop their interests and practical skills in cookery, engineering, construction or textiles.

> (Ofsted 2011a)

After visits to secondary schools (11–19 years), similar messages were reported. Conclusions were that students produced outstanding achievements when they:

- demonstrated commitment to acquiring, analysing and applying knowledge
- were productive, demonstrated good management and efficient use of time, including use of computers to aid design and manufacture
- worked constructively with others and managed risks well to manufacture products safely
- responded to ambitious challenges, showing significant originality or creativity, and produced varied and innovative ideas and manufactured prototypes
- had opportunities to acquire a secure understanding of the properties of materials and use them with increasing confidence to undertake innovative or unusual design and making.

(Ofsted 2011b)

This report made considerable impact beyond schools, with *The Engineer* (2011) publishing the following comments:

> The world faces a huge shortage of engineers with hands-on experience designing, making and using modern tools such as CAD/CAM, electronics and control systems . . . Exciting and imaginative D&T teaching in school will be crucial for our future success.
>
> (The author was a talent resourcing manager
> for a multinational industrial group)

And

> Now is the time to stop our children being channelled by a constraining curriculum into making weather vanes and CD racks, and to begin taking on projects that stimulate creativity, focusing on those borne out of product need, problem solving and sustainability.
>
> (Royal Academy of Engineering 2011)

Further observations of the value of real-world examples are included in the reports of other initiatives, for example, the 2011 evaluation report for the STEMNET programme (Straw *et al.* 2011). This report emphasised the importance of STEM clubs and interactions with STEM ambassadors in increasing students' interest in STEM and developing their subject knowledge and practical and transferable skills, such as team-working and problem-solving – all of which are important in future employability.

The widescale adoption of such curriculum enrichment and enhancement activities is at the core of the school-based targets in the current UK STEM Programme (discussed later in this chapter).

Ideas and advice about developing a rich programme of STEM activities, within and beyond the classroom, are explored in further detail in following chapters.

STEM literacy

Mastery of the three Rs – reading, writing and arithmetic – has been recognised as an essential objective in education for over a century. Literacy and numeracy are the terms frequently used to describe these competencies.

Recognition of the dependence of successful industries on the STEM skills of the workforce and the need for individuals both to understand technological and medical advances (and their social and environmental impacts) and to be able to use STEM skills in their everyday lives, has led to the concept of an additional competence, referred to as 'STEM literacy'.

Nobel laureate Sir Harry Kroto supports the call for universal scientific literacy:

> As well as trained engineers and scientists, we desperately need a scientifically literate general population, capable of thinking rationally – and that includes lawyers, business-people, farmers, politicians, journalists and athletes. This is vital if we are to secure a sustainable world for our grandchildren.
>
> (Kroto 2007)

The importance of STEM literacy across society is recognised in the USA by the National Council of Teachers of English (2013). With reference to 'twenty-first-century literacies', they note that literacy must change as society and technology change and suggest that successful participants in our twenty-first-century global society must:

- develop proficiency with the tools of technology
- build cross-cultural connections with others to solve problems collaboratively
- design and share information for global communities
- manage, analyse and synthesise multiple streams of information
- create, critique and evaluate multimedia
- attend to the ethical responsibilities required by complex environments.

Skill and expertise in STEM subjects are requirements for those engaged in STEM-based further education or training. Less recognised is the level of STEM competence required by everyone in society to make informed decisions about their everyday lives. In our rapidly changing world, new technologies constantly appear, bringing with them the need for new skills.

Development of the capacity for lifelong learning in STEM, or STEM literacy, was recognised as an essential component of STEM education in England in the 2006 STEM programme report (Department for Education and Skills 2006).

The Beyond Current Horizons (2009) research programme also discussed the need for lifelong learning, with social scientists providing insights into different possibilities that might face future education and learning. Not predictions, but stories of different possible futures, these imagined how the world might look after 2025, to challenge assumptions and stimulate thinking about the present. The final report suggested that:

- today's 'digital natives' will, like their parents before them, need to learn to use new technological environments throughout their lives
- lifelong education of adults will move to the fore alongside early learners, and education by chronological age will blur.

Employers are regularly faced with reviewing practices and adopting new processes to improve efficiency and drive up quality assurance. They are, therefore, keen to recruit a 'STEM-literate' workforce with the ability to engage with new technological processes and to adapt to changing circumstances.

The needs of industry are likely to change continually as research and development offer new opportunities. When discussing the future needs of employers, the Beyond Current Horizons report (2009) suggested that regular and continual upgrading of skills will become the norm to keep pace with technological developments and demands.

There have been numerous attempts to define STEM literacy. One of the best may be Leon Lederman's definition, as cited by Zollman (2012):

> STEM literacy . . . is the ability to adapt to and accept changes driven by new technology work, to anticipate the multilevel impacts of their actions, communicate complex ideas effectively to a variety of audiences, and perhaps most importantly, find measured yet creative solutions to problems which are today unimaginable.

The current capacity of schools to nurture STEM literacy is questioned (Pitt 2009; Williams 2011), because of the insular way in which the STEM subjects are delivered in the school curriculum. In particular they highlight:

- lack of discussion about similarities, differences, and relationships between Science, Technology, Engineering and Maths as school subjects
- lack of clarity about similarities, differences and relationships between STEM, scientific and technological literacy
- problems with regard to educational outcomes and success criteria.

Education policy makers accept STEM literacy as a desired outcome of successful STEM education at schools and colleges in the UK. However, there is little enunciation of what the success criteria are.

Despite investment in shaping the nature of new STEM initiatives and in the implementation of intervention strategies for targeted audiences, evaluation studies have been primarily quantitative rather than qualitative. This makes them better suited to measuring impact on people entering STEM careers and further education rather than measuring increase in capacity for STEM literacy.

In preparation for writing, the authors spent a considerable amount of time consulting educational professionals and other STEM stakeholders to develop their own understanding of 'what successful STEM education is' and our resulting views and beliefs underpin the observations and recommendations presented here.

STEM skills

With the UK being the world's sixth largest manufacturer, with an engineering turnover of around £800 billion per year, STEM subjects are clearly integral to the UK's success. Whilst the UK makes up only 1 per cent of the world's population, it produces 10 per cent of the world's top scientific research (National STEM Centre 2013a).

Each year, the Confederation of British Industry surveys members about their preferences for education and skills levels of existing and new employees. The 2012 report, from 540 employers and 1.6 million employees, suggested serious shortfalls in the availability of recruits with STEM-related experience and expertise.

Reported shortages in STEM skills were widespread. Of employers surveyed, 42 per cent reported difficulty in recruiting staff and 45 per cent expected difficulty in the next 3 years. Employers also reported that 20 per cent of jobs now required a degree, with 50 per cent of employers favouring STEM degrees.

Current numbers of students and apprentices following STEM courses in further and higher education are insufficient to meet projected recruitment needs of industry. A major contributory factor is the small proportion of students choosing to study STEM subjects beyond the age of compulsory study. Attention has, therefore, turned to how schools might encourage more students to consider STEM careers.

In 2012, Professor Sir John Beddington and Dame Nancy Rothwell, co-chairs of the Council for Science and Technology, wrote an open letter to the Prime Minister emphasising the role of education in supplying highly skilled, creative workers for UK industry and academia:

> an excellent Science, Technology, Engineering and Maths (STEM) education system that produces our future scientists and engineers, and equips the public to understand emerging technologies . . . is critical to our future economic growth.
>
> (Beddington and Rothwell 2012)

Shortage of recruits with STEM skills is not a new phenomenon. Sir Gareth Roberts reviewed the factors influencing the supply of Science and Engineering skills in the UK as part of the government's strategy for improving UK productivity and innovation. His report, SET for Success (Roberts 2002) warned that the future productivity and competitiveness of the UK economy was inexorably linked to the availability of scientists, engineers and technologists (Figure 1.1).

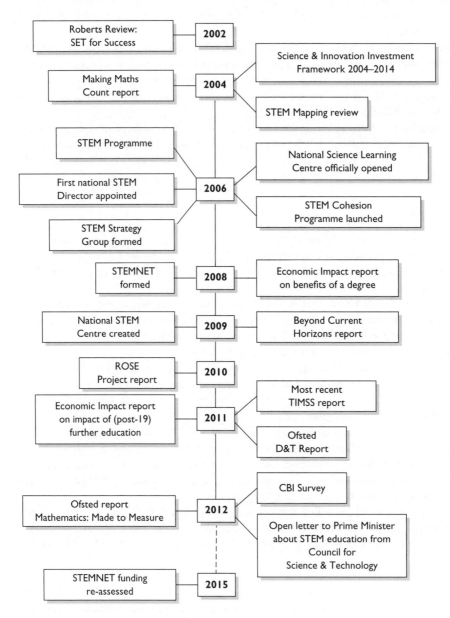

Figure 1.1 Timeline of some key STEM events, important for UK schools and mentioned in this chapter.

Although employing the acronym SET (Science, Engineering and Technology) in the title of the report and with headlines focusing on these three areas, the requirement for Maths skills was acknowledged throughout the report and resulting action plans contained explicit targets for Maths education and training.

The Roberts report noted a mismatch between the demands of industry for graduates of Mathematics, Engineering and Physical Sciences and the number of students studying these subjects in university, despite enhanced employment and salary prospects for such graduates. Areas of biological and medical science research were also reported as being at risk due to reduced numbers of graduates with physical science backgrounds.

STEM BEYOND SCHOOL

In a European Commission survey of European attitudes towards Science and Technology it was found that:

- 76 per cent of Europeans agreed that, even if it brings no immediate benefits, scientific research, which adds to knowledge, should be supported by government.
- 64 per cent appreciated that advanced technologies are needed for their economy to be competitive.
- 48 per cent believed in science and technological developments and that new inventions would counteract any harmful effects. These responses were polarised, e.g. 76 per cent of Poles believed this, but only 20 per cent of Danes, 22 per cent of UK citizens and 26 per cent of Irish (European Commission 2005).

In spite of such endorsements of the value of Science and Technology to society by EU citizens, interest by young Europeans is not comparable. In 2007 the European Commission commissioned a Flash Eurobarometer survey of over 24,500 young people, aged between 15 and 25, to determine their interest in Science and Technology and their plans for future involvement in the scientific domains.

Presented with several choices of future science-related study areas, only a minority said they were considering them. The most popular areas to study were Social Sciences, then Economics or Business Studies, with Mathematics being least favoured. Other findings from the survey included the following:

- In all EU Member States, less than half of young people were considering studying Natural Sciences, ranging from 47 per cent (Slovenia) to 13 per cent (UK).
- In each EU Member State, less than half were thinking of studying Mathematics, ranging from 41 per cent (Lithuania) to 16 per cent (Austria).
- Young men were more likely to consider courses in Engineering or Mathematics than women (39 per cent compared to 16 per cent).
- Most young women considering studying Natural Science or Mathematics did so with the expectation of becoming a health professional, a teacher or a public sector researcher.
- Most young men considering studying Natural Science or Mathematics expected to become engineers, technicians or researchers in the private sector (Gallup Organization 2009).

Table 1.1 Factors affecting numbers studying STEM (Roberts 2002)

At school	At university
Relative shortage of girls studying A-level Maths and Physical Sciences (particularly Physics and Engineering)	Insufficiently attractive career opportunities compared to other sectors
Poor experiences of Science and Engineering education	Lack of transferable skills and knowledge, due to teaching methods
Negative images of careers linked to studying Science and Engineering	

Another significant finding was that, by the age of 15, the youngest age category in this survey, young people in Ireland and the UK appeared the most likely to give 'already chosen a profession' as their reason for not considering Engineering, Biology or Medicine.

Evidence from the Eurobarometer survey reinforces other messages from the UK, for example, from the 2002 Roberts review, and indicates the need for STEM careers information, advice and guidance from an early age. STEM careers education is explored in Chapter 6.

As part of the extensive Roberts review, STEM teaching methods and curricula in schools and universities were examined to try and find out why so few students chose STEM subjects post-16 and even fewer chose STEM-related degree courses. Table 1.1 shows the factors that were identified.

Around this time, Professor Adrian Smith chaired an independent inquiry into post-14 Mathematics education, complementing the Roberts report of Science and Engineering. The Making Mathematics Count inquiry (Smith 2004) concluded that Mathematics:

- provides the underpinning language for Science and Engineering and, increasingly, for disciplines in social and medical sciences
- underpins business and industry, in particular, financial services and ICT
- provides citizens with empowering skills in their private and social lives.

This highlighted the importance of mathematical capability, not just as an essential life skill, but also as a key skill required at virtually all levels of employment (Smith 2004).

Early initiatives to increase numbers of people with STEM skills

Roberts' and Smith's reports galvanised the UK government and STEM stakeholders, such as educational charities, professional institutions and bodies, to respond with a range of initiatives. This resulted in a huge growth in materials and resources for schools to try and raise the quantity and quality of STEM enrichment and engagement.

Whilst generally welcomed, the volume of resources, activities and training courses developed and promoted by separate stakeholders created some bemusement and confusion amongst many of the intended beneficiaries in schools and colleges. There was also duplication of effort, as organisations were not liaising sufficiently with each other.

To establish the extent of the initiatives available to schools, the STEM mapping review (Department for Education 2004) collated information about all the STEM support

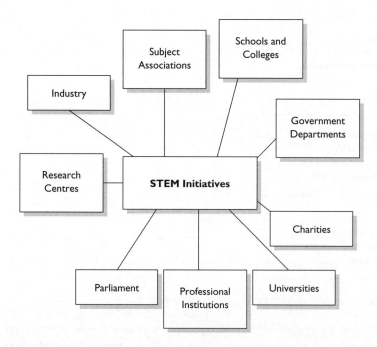

Figure 1.2 Main types of stakeholders in the STEM mapping review.

materials and activities produced on behalf of government departments, agencies and other stakeholders. Over 470 major initiatives were identified, with around 200 originating from the government (Figure 1.2).

Also in 2004, the government published the Science and Innovation Investment Framework, 2004–2014 (HM Treasury 2004). This ten-year framework recognised the importance of increasing the supply of people with STEM skills. This included improving the:

- quality of Science teachers in every school
- results for students studying Science at age 16
- numbers choosing STEM subjects for post-16 education and beyond.

Promotion of STEM in schools and colleges

As part of the Science and Innovation Investment Framework, 2004–2014, the government set up the Science, Technology, Engineering and Mathematics (STEM) Programme (Figure 1.1) to rationalise the range of STEM initiatives and to create a national strategy to provide STEM support for schools (Department for Education 2006).

Another outcome of the framework was the formation of a STEM strategy group with responsibility for all phases of STEM education and for making recommendations about national STEM priorities. Professor John Holman, based at the National Science Learning Centre in York, was appointed as National STEM Director. Shortly afterwards, he launched the national STEM Cohesion Programme with the priorities shown in Figure 1.3.

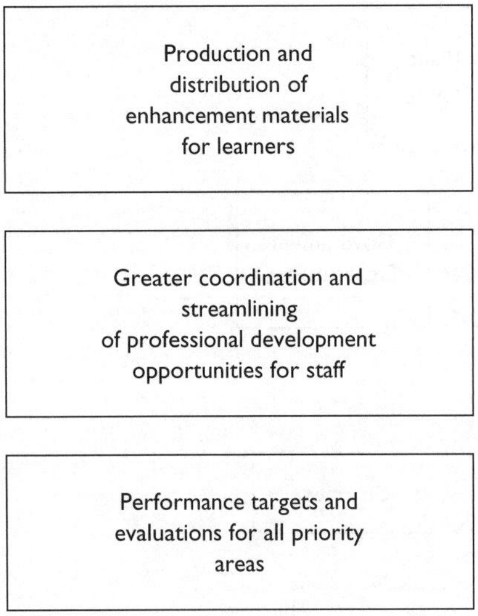

```
┌─────────────────────────────┐
│      Production and          │
│      distribution of         │
│   enhancement materials      │
│       for learners           │
└─────────────────────────────┘

┌─────────────────────────────┐
│   Greater coordination and   │
│        streamlining          │
│  of professional development │
│    opportunities for staff   │
└─────────────────────────────┘

┌─────────────────────────────┐
│   Performance targets and    │
│   evaluations for all priority│
│           areas              │
└─────────────────────────────┘
```

Figure 1.3 Priorities of the national STEM Cohesion Programme.

The simplified Cohesion Programme of STEM support was intended to be cost-neutral to the Treasury. The benefits of collaborative marketing and the elimination of duplicated resources were expected to offset the costs of setting up the new infrastructure. It was also anticipated that the support offered to schools and colleges would be:

- more accessible
- branded more identifiably
- better signposted.

It should therefore be easier for schools to select the most relevant and useful materials for their specific needs.

DELIVERY OF STEM ACTION PLANS

The STEM Cohesion Programme, which operated until 2010, identified five key target areas, shown in Figure 1.4.

Each of the key target areas had one or more Action Plans. Lead organisations were nominated to rationalise current initiatives and to coordinate future initiatives for each of the 11 Action Plans.

The role of schools in developing STEM skills

STEM education can contribute to the development of students' personal, learning and thinking skills as well as their understanding of how modern society has developed. Making STEM integral to the curriculum provides many contexts for rich learning experiences.

Figure 1.5 shows how STEM enrichment opportunities can link to the aims of the National Curriculum for England (Department for Education 2012c).

Target Area	Action Plan	Lead Organisation
Recruit highly qualified STEM teachers	1: Getting the right people to become teachers and lecturers	The Training and Development Agency for Schools
Increase the quality of STEM teaching by providing professional development for teachers	2: Improving teaching and learning through continuing professional development for Mathematics teachers	The National Centre for Excellence in the Teaching of Mathematics
	3: Improving teaching and learning through continuing professional development for Science teachers	The National Science Learning Centre
	4: Improving teaching and learning by engaging teachers in Technology and Engineering	The Royal Academy of Engineering
Build stronger links between schools and real world applications of STEM; improve careers advice.	5: Bringing real-world context and applications of STEM into schools to enrich the teaching of science	SCORE (Science Community Representing Education)
	6: Bringing real-world context and applications of STEM into schools to enrich the teaching of Technology and Engineering	Royal Academy of Engineering
	7: Bringing real-world context and applications of STEM into schools to enrich the teaching of Mathematics	Advisory Committee on Mathematics Education
	8: Improving the quality of advice and guidance for students, teachers and parents about STEM careers	The National STEM Careers Coordinator, Kate Bellingham
Improve the STEM curriculum to raise exam results at age 16; increase take up of STEM subjects post-16; increase the quality of practical work	9: Widening access to the formal Science and Mathematics curriculum for all students, including access to Triple Science	Department for Children, Schools and Families
	10: Improving the quality of practical work in Science	SCORE
Improve the STEM infrastructure	11: Building capacity of national, regional and local infrastructures	Department for Children, Schools and Families

Figure 1.4 Target areas of the STEM Cohesion Programme.

The National Curriculum for Scotland (Education Scotland 2011) shares the aims of the English Curriculum, but lists a fourth aim: 'effective contributors'. This more inclusive expression about successful learners fits particularly well with the rationale and methodology of many styles of STEM engagement.

One way of assessing the effectiveness of Science and Maths education is to compare the academic achievement of students from countries across the world.

The Trends in International Mathematics and Science Study, TIMSS (Table 1.2), has measured trends in Maths and Science achievements of 9- and 13-year-olds in 63 different countries, every 4 years since 1995. Table 1.2 shows some of the results for the fifth study in 2011.

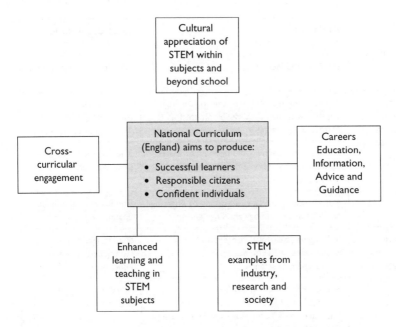

Figure 1.5 STEM enrichment links to aims of the National Curriculum.

Table 1.2 Trends in International Maths and Science Study (TIMSS) 2011 results for students in England

	Ranking out of 63 countries	
	9-year-olds	13-year-olds
Maths	9th	10th
Science	15th	9th

These results are of concern due to England's position in relation to global industrial and commercial competitors. In Maths, most of the countries ranking higher were in the Pacific Rim, including Chinese Taipei, South Korea, Singapore, Hong Kong and Japan. Maths scores for 9-year-olds indicate little change in relative position since 2007, suggesting a tailing-off in improvement after a rapid increase from 1995. There have been no significant changes in the performances of 13-year-olds in Maths from 1995 to 2011.

In Science, the attainment of 9-year-old students in England has declined since 2007 after a period of improvement from 1995 to 2003 and stability from 2003 to 2007. This decline coincides with the ending of mandatory Key Stage 2 tests in Science in 2009, but whether there is a link is not known. TIMSS show no significant changes in attainment in Science for 13-year-olds in England since 1995.

Analysis of TIMSS produces some interesting observations about attainment of male and female students in England. No gender differences are seen in Mathematics for either age group or in Science for students aged 9 years during the study. Gender differences in Science at age 13 persisted until the 2003 study, but have since been eradicated.

Another international study, the Relevance of Science Education (ROSE) project investigated students' attitudes and motivation towards Science and Technology, so

Table 1.3 Gender attitudes towards careers, summarised from Jenkins and Pell (2006)

STEM area and/or career aspirations	More important for girls	More important for boys	About equal importance to boys and girls
Helping other people	✓		
Working with people rather than things	✓		
Becoming famous		✓	
Working with technology and mechanics		✓	
Working with animals			✓
Having time for family			✓
Using their talents and abilities			✓

complementing TIMSS. Sjøberg and Schreiner (2010) explained the importance of the findings of the ROSE project as follows:

- Positive attitudes towards Science and Technology are important.
- Knowledge matters, but so does a cultural appreciation for Science and Technology.
- Values and interest in Science and Technology are important determinants for future educational choices and behaviour as citizens.
- When facts, concepts and theories of school Science are forgotten, the 'ethos' or 'atmosphere' of the subject remains and shapes behaviour, interests and attitudes in adult life. Bad experiences with Science and Mathematics have lasting detrimental effects; positive experiences are likely to have lasting positive effects.

Some gender attitudes towards careers of 15-year-old UK students, from the ROSE project, are summarised in Table 1.3.

Further analysis of the ROSE project showed that UK students compared unfavourably with those from other EU countries in terms of their interest in STEM (Sjøberg and Schreiner 2010). Figure 1.6 illustrates this comparison.

For STEM teachers across the UK, this is bleak news. Many of the STEM promotional initiatives in the UK were started soon after the Roberts review in 2002, which means that the 15-year-olds who were the focus of the 2010 ROSE report would have received most of their secondary education in an era awash with STEM intervention initiatives.

The ROSE project report (Sjøberg and Schreiner 2010) suggests that a significant gulf remains between the aspirations of STEM educators and the attitudes towards STEM expressed by young people in the UK. This negativity towards STEM is also evident to some extent in countries with relatively high ratings on the Human Development Index (HDI). HDI is defined by the United Nations Development Programme through a composite of factors, including life expectancy at birth; adult literacy rate; combined gross enrolment ratio for primary, secondary and tertiary schools and gross domestic product per capita (United Nations Development Programme 2013).

A possible explanation of the inverse relationship between HDI and attitudes could be that students in countries with high HDI take the benefits of Science and Technology for granted as they are part of daily life, unlike students in low HDI countries, who do not have the 'luxuries' associated with highly developed technological societies.

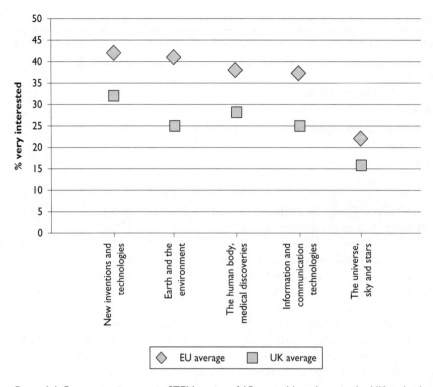

Figure 1.6 Percentage interest in STEM topics of 15-year-old students in the UK and other EU countries.

Other messages from the ROSE project show significant differences in attitudes depending on the areas of the curriculum under consideration. Gender differences in attitudes towards STEM have been reported in previous studies and continue to need addressing.

The role of the National STEM Centre

The national network of ten Science Learning Centres provides exciting, and often subsidised (via Enthuse bursaries), professional development for those working with students aged 5 to 19 in Science and D&T, including:

- primary and secondary teachers
- post-16/further education teachers and lecturers
- teaching assistants
- technicians.

Establishment of a national network was a massive investment in professional development for Science and Technology staff in response to the growing needs identified by the Roberts review (2002). The professional development framework provided by the

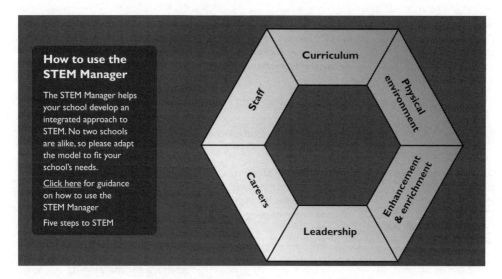

How to use the STEM Manager

The STEM Manager helps your school develop an integrated approach to STEM. No two schools are alike, so please adapt the model to fit your school's needs.

Click here for guidance on how to use the STEM Manager

Five steps to STEM

Curriculum

Physical environment

Staff

Careers

Enhancement & enrichment

Leadership

Figure 1.7 The free, online STEM Manager tool from the National STEM Centre.

network of Science Learning Centres was central to meeting targets of the 2006 STEM Cohesion Programme, particularly Action Plan 3 (Figure 1.4), which was 'Improving teaching and learning through continuing professional development for Science teachers'.

In 2009, the National STEM Centre was founded within the existing National Science Learning Centre at York University. Funded by the Gatsby Charitable Foundation, the National STEM Centre now houses the UK's largest collection of STEM teaching and learning resources. Its virtual e-library provides publications and media resources to support STEM teaching in schools. The archive is a growing repository of older materials available for consultation.

Another online service offered by the National STEM Centre is a suite of STEM planning tools (National STEM Centre 2013b). These can support school staff in planning and mapping STEM activities for learners of different ages and across traditional subject boundaries, not just STEM, but increasingly IT and programming. Prompts to enter information and visual representations of stored data make planning integrated STEM provision both within and outside the curriculum easier and give an overview of opportunities provided to students.

The STEM Manager tool (Figure 1.7) includes areas to record the demand on staffing and facilities to support curriculum enrichment activities. It is a very useful resource for STEM leaders and coordinators.

STEMNET

The schools' STEM Advisory Network, STEMNET, provides a free advisory service to schools and teachers of students up to the age of 19. A network of contract holders across the UK aims to ensure that all schools and colleges can offer programmes which support the curriculum and increase the quality and quantity of students moving into further STEM education, training and development. Funding for STEMNET is assured until 2015 by the Department for Business, Innovation and Skills.

Little or no uptake of STEM E&E events or activities made available by schools	Occasional involvement in STEM E&E but ad hoc and little coordination across STEM subjects	STEM E&E planning integrated into school life, involvement encouraged and celebrated by whole school community

Level of adoption of STEM philosophy within schools

Students see no examples of STEM applications/meet no STEM role models apart from circle of friends and family	Some students get access to opportunities and may meet STEM role models but impact is limited by events being presented in isolation	Students experience a rich variety of STEM E&E events and activities across subjects throughout their school lives. STEM ambassadors used to enhance curriculum delivery, act as role models and support careers events

Figure 1.8 Levels of adoption of STEM philosophy within schools.

Local contacts regularly meet with secondary staff to assess requirements and to provide impartial and tailored advice to enrich and enhance student STEM experiences. Teachers can then coordinate activities of greatest benefit to their students by using STEMNET's strong links with businesses and partner organisations.

The brokerage, or advice and guidance service, offered by STEMNET is rated highly by teachers. A 2011 evaluation showed that more than three-quarters (77 per cent) of teachers who had engaged with STEMNET rated the experience as 'very useful' or 'useful'. However, research conducted for the evaluation suggested more could be done to make schools aware of the service and support available. This recommendation was taken forward and is part of STEMNET's 2011–2015 remit in working with schools.

STEMNET's goal is to achieve a high level of STEM E&E work as an integrated component within all schools in the UK. Currently it is recognised that STEM engagement varies widely between schools (Figure 1.8).

One of the key services offered by STEMNET is the STEM ambassadors programme. Over 25,000 volunteers offer time and support to promote STEM subjects to students. With experiences of STEM research, industry and/or academia, STEM ambassadors work with teachers, helping them deliver the STEM curriculum in relevant and engaging ways. They also contribute to informal STEM enrichment, for example, by mentoring project work carried out in extracurricular clubs.

The evaluation report of 'the impact of STEMNET's services on pupils and teachers' (National Foundation for Educational Research 2011) indicated that teachers were generally very positive about STEM ambassadors:

- 86 per cent reported increased student engagement and interest in STEM subjects.
- 83 per cent reported increased knowledge and understanding of subjects/concepts/topics.
- 67 per cent reported an increased awareness of the STEM employment and career options available.

When questioned about any impact of STEM ambassadors on their personal professional development:

- 69 per cent of teachers cited 'increased ability to relate lessons to real world applications of the subjects'.
- 67 per cent suggested that they had gained confidence/motivation/enthusiasm/attitudes/aspirations in relation to teaching STEM subjects.

Despite encouraging feedback, there are questions about the overall impact of STEM ambassadors. Most schools have more contact with ambassadors in Science and/or in D&T than in Maths or Engineering. STEMNET contractors for the current phase of the programme (2011–2015) therefore have targets to recruit and deploy a more representative cohort of ambassadors.

Another key service offered by STEMNET is STEM clubs support. STEM clubs can allow students to investigate and discover STEM subjects in stimulating learning environments, away from timetable constraints or a prescribed curriculum. STEM clubs may follow themes integrating STEM aspects, but in the UK, clubs offering experiences in single areas, such as Astronomy or Zoology, are also referred to as 'STEM clubs'.

The UK government funded After-School Science and Engineering Clubs (ASSECs) from 2007 to 2009. At least two members of staff per school, from different STEM teaching areas, were required to attend training as a condition of the funding. The 500 clubs that received funding used it for additional equipment, transport to STEM events and, in some instances, extra payments for technicians and/or staff involved in delivering STEM club activities.

Following this 'golden age' of generous funding, the principle of STEM clubs was rolled out to the remaining 3,000 or so secondary schools, with the expectation that they would emulate the activities of the funded pilot ASSECs, benefiting from the resources shared by pilot clubs on the official STEMClubs website, but 'funded through existing means'.

Some funding was released for part-time STEM club advisors to support clubs registering with the STEMClubs website, but in 2012 responsibility for STEM clubs was passed from the British Science Association to STEMNET and the club support to schools became an additional remit for local STEMNET contractors. STEMNET offers free, bespoke advice to staff in schools about launching new STEM clubs or about refreshing established clubs.

Chapters 4 and 5 have more information about STEM clubs.

STEM education in the UK: a progress report

STEM education was recognised as a major priority for schools in the 2007 McKinsey report (McKinsey & Co 2007). An important, but perhaps not surprising, finding from this report was that top-performing school 'systems' ultimately depend on the quality of the teachers.

A measure of the success of STEM initiatives comes from a Department for Education (2011) report. This reported increased percentages of students taking A-level (post-16) exams in many STEM subjects.

Key figures showed:

- 12 per cent rise in Maths entries in 2009, and a further 8 per cent rise in 2010
- 10 per cent increase in Biology entries in 2010

- 9 per cent increase in Chemistry entries in 2010
- 8 per cent rise in Physics entries in 2010.

It makes sense that, to succeed in STEM subjects, learners need strong subject teaching, including specialist knowledge to challenge and inspire them. Teachers who are passionate about their subject and effective in creating enthusiastic learners are vital if students are to enjoy, and achieve their maximum potential in, STEM subjects. The rest of this book aims to help you have great success with STEM in and out of the classroom.

Chapter 2

Enhancement and enrichment in STEM

Making lessons buzz

By the end of this chapter, you will have ideas about how to:

- enhance lessons to engage students
- provide exciting and rich experiences for students.

There is much advice on best practices in teaching and in subject-specific learning and teaching. This chapter aims to complement this by illustrating ways to create outstanding lessons where you and your students will learn a lot and be motivated and engaged by the process. Examples of creative lesson content are given and opportunities to enhance and extend existing resources are suggested.

The Miami Museum of Science has an inspirational webpage, about acids and alkalis, with interactive links labelled as:

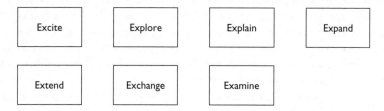

These terms are great prompts to use when planning lessons to interest and challenge your students – if these components are present, then you have a framework capable of meeting the needs of all learners and ensuring their progress during your lesson.

Other useful 'E' buzzwords that could be added to this 'checklist' include:

It is not suggested that every STEM session should have all of the above, but including one or more of these aspects ought to go a long way towards creating memorable and effective (another 'E'!) STEM lessons. The National STEM Centre particularly endorses 'enhancement and enrichment': 'Using *enhancement* and *enrichment* activities helps to promote greater *engagement* with *STEM* subjects' (National STEM Centre 2000–2009).

Giving students some structured 'ownership' of lesson content, such as an element of choice, is often a key factor in students' engagement. Research suggests a positive link between choice and levels of motivation (McCombs undated, and Pintrich 2003, amongst others). Ownership can promote learners' personal interest and so build motivation and confidence. Encouraging exploration of new ideas, along with an element of 'risk-taking', can also help provide an exciting climate for learning, as students are challenged to be creative alongside their knowledge and understanding of the STEM topic.

Professor Ainissa Ramirez, Yale University, makes the point that learners today need to be able to 'think expansively and solve problems resourcefully' (Ramirez 2013). Along with calling for a recommitment to improve STEM education in (US) schools, Ramirez describes what she believes needs to change to make STEM fun again. This includes increasing every student's participation in STEM by encouraging:

- collaboration
- communication
- creativity
- critical thinking
- curiosity
- cracking problems.

The above attributes or skills are vital for citizens and scientists. They not only relate to public understanding of STEM, but are principles of research.

Tytler *et al.* (2008) believe that students need challenge and exposure to ideas that they 'can engage with at high level' and Blatchford (2013) recommends 'the promotion of scholarship' to make teaching inspiring and vibrant. By using suggestions from this book, we hope that you feel empowered to create the sorts of learning environments in which your students believe that they can and will succeed with challenges that help them realise their potential.

The rest of this chapter provides suggestions and examples for embedding some of the above ideas within lessons. As great lessons are rooted in teachers' excellent subject knowledge and passion, Chapter 3 gives some ideas about where and how teachers of STEM subjects can find help with professional development.

Making lessons buzz

When 12-year-old students from schools in Oxford were asked what made their Science lessons inspiring, Wilson and Mant (2011) found that the lessons of the most positive and enthusiastic students were characterised by:

- teachers who explain clearly
- student opportunities for practical work
- opportunities for thinking, problem-solving and discussions
- the subject presented in context.

These results build upon a considerable body of earlier research (Barmby *et al.* 2008; Osborne and Dillon 2008) and it is not unreasonable to suggest that similar results might be expected for other STEM subjects. The value of such evidence should give teachers confidence that: 'facilitating discussions, encouraging thinking and delivering practical science in a manner that related it to everyday life is indeed an 'essential' and not a luxury or an add-on' (Wilson and Mant 2011).

Effective use of current events

Current events bring the outside world into the STEM classroom. They can:

- act as a 'hook' or stimulus material to engage curiosity
- launch class discussions
- increase the relevance of a topic
- increase interest and motivation.

A search through online or paper newspapers shows that most pages contain one or more links to a STEM topic. These can be used for any of the purposes listed above.

Table 2.1 has examples from the Guardian online, on the day that the first draft of this chapter was written. These were just the first found; many more could have been included.

Creating a display board of newspaper articles that link to curriculum areas can be rewarding. A 'Science in the News' board was successful in one school, partly due to positioning next to where students queued to enter a classroom, so it gave students something to read while they waited. The success was also due to students being providers of some articles: being 'paid' with one 'credit' per article used encouraged participation. To sustain attraction, 'STEM in the News' displays must be current, so refreshing content regularly is important.

Table 2.1 News items, 19 February 2013, linked to STEM topics

Article	Suggested STEM links
UK horsemeat tests	**Food technology:** food regulations and labelling
	Biology: DNA; genetic fingerprinting; gel electrophoresis; animal genomes; species; food tests
	Chemistry: organic chemistry, particularly proteins
	Maths: significance of percentages of products contaminated; probability of any health effects; analysis of data
	Primary Science: classification
Chinese army unit 'behind hacking'	**Maths:** appreciation of numbers (terabytes, etc.)
	Computer Science: hacking – what it is and the issues surrounding it
Nuclear reactor deals 'to last to 2050'	**Physics:** nuclear power, alternative energies
Review blasts Australian swim team	**Biology:** use and abuse of drugs
	Physics/Primary Science: shapes and streamlining; flow and resistance in water
	Maths: calculations of speed

Some guides to help use current events in STEM lessons include:

- *Front-Page Science: Engaging Teens in Science Literacy* (Saul *et al.* 2011)
- Extra! Extra! Read all about Science: a blog (Bridges 2012)
- Teaching Kids News: website with a strong focus on Technology
- Mathematics news via the Science Daily news website.

Sparking and stimulating curiosity

Ramirez (2013) believes that encouraging curiosity is a key way of increasing student participation in STEM. This builds on research (Mitchell 1993; Jenkins and Nelson 2005) that suggests students who perceive themselves as active learners have greater interest than those who are passive absorbers of knowledge.

Using the following approaches can introduce problems for students to tackle and attempt to solve:

- Enquiry/inquiry-based learning – this is a student-centred, active learning approach focusing on questioning, critical thinking and problem-solving (note: 'enquiry' tends to be UK spelling, 'inquiry' US spelling).
- Problem-based learning – also a student-centred, active learning approach but focusing on the process of solving a problem, often a 'real-world' issue. Students identify what they already know and what they need to learn, then they apply knowledge to try and solve the problem.
- Imaginative inquiry is based upon the idea that the greatest resource in a classroom is student imagination. Mainly used up to age 11, the idea could be adapted for use with older students. With this approach, students can be anyone, at any time, anywhere, doing anything, such as Egyptian engineers working on the Pyramids. This could also link well into promoting STEM careers, where students could be encouraged to imagine being an astronomer or microbiologist.

Since questions or challenges can be as short or as long as wanted, they can fit into part of a lesson or make the basis of a project running over several lessons. CREST Award schemes (see Box 2.2 on page 35) are worth considering in this context.

Once students learn how to question and discover new information themselves, they should be more able to think independently and critically, increasing their chances of success both in and beyond school.

Choosing the right question to start any discovery learning (as all three approaches may be described) needs careful thought to ensure sparking the curiosity of the students. Good questions are likely to build on prior knowledge to provide students with a starting point. Some examples, with potential for success, include:

- How can you defeat a dragon with Maths? (Sundem undated)
- How did Felix Baumgartner jump from the edge of space and survive?
- How do visual illusions work?
- How can tablets be protected from accidental damage?

Some inspiring work by 10–11-year-olds was reported at an Association for Science Education annual conference (Spalding 2012). Students were asked what questions they would like to investigate. With a little help, the students were able to investigate their own questions and arrive at answers. This shows that even young students can be researchers.

The idea of letting students frame their own questions is endorsed by the authors of *Make Just One Change: Teach Students to Ask Their Own Questions* (Rothstein and Santana 2011). The authors say that, when teachers deploy this approach, it causes three changes:

1   increased participation in group and peer learning processes
2   improved classroom management
3   enhanced efforts to address inequities in education.

Stimulus material for sparking students' curiosity could come from special days, weeks or events. These could be particular to the school or local area, or national or international events. A year's worth of suggestions are given by Scott and Howarth (2011) and Howarth and Scott (2011b). Although dates change slightly each year for most of these, it is easy to find out current dates. Anniversary dates of STEM figures and events, of course, never change and the History section that follows has ideas about using these.

Using projects, debates, history, drama and culture

Using variety within lessons provides opportunities to meet the attributes that Ramirez (2013) suggests are necessary for students to enjoy and participate in STEM subjects (collaboration, creativity, critical thinking, curiosity and cracking problems.) Tack the likelihood of challenges and the need for good communication skills on to that list, as well as almost certain elements of choice, and you have a recipe for a successful lesson in which students make progress.

Projects and investigations

These can be fantastic for enhancement and enrichment opportunities. Once a project or investigation has been trialled, it is always easier to repeat, amend and extend. Any extra efforts needed in setting up projects for the first time may be repaid when recycled for use with new students.

Chapter 5 has information about projects in STEM clubs and Chapter 11 has ideas for project titles across the STEM disciplines. Most projects and investigations offer opportunities for students to:

• become better independent learners
• develop and apply problem-solving skills
• enhance planning, research, data collection, analysis, evaluation and presentation skills
• extend knowledge and understanding of a topic
• develop creativity and initiative
• develop personal ownership and hence deeper interest and involvement
• make choices and so generate intrinsic motivation.

Project-based learning has become more common in schools, particularly in the USA, where some schools use nothing but this approach. Mitchell *et al.* (2009) discuss this further.

There are many sources of advice about running school projects and investigations, including advice from examination boards. The Guardian Teacher Network has some good advice on launching projects, e.g. environmental projects (Drury 2012) and renewable energy projects (Clarke 2013).

Debates

Many STEM topics involve social, ethical, economical and environmental issues, so offer opportunities to hold lively debates. Debates need not be long or formal. Short, focused debates can be effective, particularly if students have researched a topic and collated information in advance.

Under the current National Curriculum, 2008 (in process of review), students aged 11–13/14 years should be taught within Science lessons to:

- explore how the creative application of scientific ideas can bring about technological developments and changes in the way people think and behave
- examine the ethical and moral implications of using and applying Science.

And students aged 13/14–16 years should be taught:

- about the use of contemporary scientific and technological developments and their benefits, drawbacks and risks
- to consider how and why decisions about Science and Technology are made, including those that raise ethical issues, and about the social, economic and environmental effects of such decisions.

A first place to look for help with debates might be your school's English department.

Finding someone to help run a debate is also possible with the free online STEM Directories. These are a resource for teachers to search for external providers to help supplement classroom activities. STEM ambassadors (see Chapter 1) are another possibility.

History

Engaging STEM lessons can arise from studying and celebrating successes from the past. This could be through historical figures, e.g. Table 2.2, or by discussing historical events, inventions, artefacts and ideas.

Commercial actors will visit schools as Brunel, Einstein, Galileo, Mendeleev and other historical figures. These liven up lessons and provide opportunities for students to question the actors about the context of their work. The internet or adverts in professional journals will help source actors. If funds are tight and you feel confident, consider dressing up or taking the part of a character yourself. Or just put on an accent! A Food Technology lesson, where the teacher taught about pasteurisation and Louis Pasteur with a French accent, was well received by the students.

Knowing dates of births, deaths and events provides opportunities for:

- short activities, e.g. a 'designer of the day' starter activity
- long activities, e.g. a main lesson activity, such as a practical based on Ohm's law
- projects, e.g. investigating a process linked to a specific person such as Pasteur.

Most days have something special associated with them, so forward planning is easy. Wikipedia lists events, births and deaths for each day of the year. Table 2.3 gives an example of STEM-related events you can find by searching a specific date.

Table 2.2 Some historical STEM figures. This is clearly not a complete list, and excludes living people, but could act as stimulus material. Several who appear could have been put in more than one category. You could have fun disagreeing with the selected names and/or ask students to come up with alternatives. It could also make the focus of a debate if you had to come up with a 'top five' or similar.

Putting historical figures from different STEM disciplines in columns like this also allows you to see whose lives overlapped – this could lead to discussions, e.g. of the contexts that contributed towards these people's achievements and the general 'invisibility' of women

Science	Technology	Engineering	Maths
Galileo Galilei 1564–1642 Astronomy	**Leonardo da Vinci** 1452–1519 Inventor and polymath	**Archimedes** 287–212BC Inventions, including gearing	**Euclid** Around 3000BC 'Father' of geometry, proof of theorems
William Harvey 1578–1657 Circulation of the blood	**Benjamin Franklin** 1706–1790 Lightning rod etc.	**John Smeaton** 1724–1792 'Father' of civil engineering	**Pythagoras of Samos** 570–494BC approx. Trigonometry
Carl Linnaeus 1707–1778 Binomial nomenclature	**Louis Pasteur** 1822–1895 Food preservation	**James Watt** 1736–1819 Mechanical engineer	**Leonardo Fibonacci** 1170–1250 Fibonacci series
Charles Darwin 1809–1882 Theory of evolution	**Thomas Crapper** 1836–1910 Toilet cisterns	**George Stephenson** 1781–1848 First intercity railway	**René Descartes** 1596–1650 Cartesian geometry/graphs
Gregor Mendel 1822–1884 Genetics	**Thomas Edison** 1847–1931 Light bulbs	**Michael Faraday** 1791–1867 Electromagnetic induction	**Isaac Newton** 1642–1727 Calculus
Dmitri Mendeleev 1834–1907 Periodic table	**Mary Anderson** 1866–1953 Windscreen wipers	**Isambard Kingdom Brunel** 1806–1859 Civil engineer	**Leonhard Euler** 1707–1783 Mathematical notation
Marie Curie 1867–1934 Radiation research	**Orville and Wilbur Wright** 1871–1948 1867–1912 First sustained flight	**Gustave Eiffel** 1832–1923 Civil engineer and architect	**Ada Lovelace** 1815–1852 First computer program
Konrad Lorentz 1903–1989 Animal behaviour	**Wallace Carothers** 1896–1937 Nylon	**Ellen Richards** 1842–1911 Environmental engineer	**Sofia Kovalevskaya** 1850–1891 Partial differential equations
Dorothy Hodgkin 1910–1994 Protein crystallography	**Bette Graham** 1924–1980 Liquid paper	**Karl Benz** 1844–1929 The first modern automobile	**Albert Einstein** 1879–1955 Theory of relativity
Rosalind Franklin 1920–1958 Structure of DNA and viruses	**Steve Jobs** 1955–2011 iTunes and iPod	**Frank Whittle** 1907–1996 Jet engines	**Alan Turing** 1912–1954 Artificial intelligence

Table 2.3 Examples of anniversaries for 16 March from Wikipedia (accessed 21 February 2013)

Year	Event	STEM opportunity
1750	Birth of Caroline Herschel, astronomer	**Visit:** Herschel museum in Bath, UK **Science:** comets **Engineering:** telescopes and lenses
1789	Birth of Georg Ohm, German physicist	**Science:** electricity; resistance; Ohm's law **Maths:** equations
1838	Death of Nathaniel Bowditch, mathematician	**Maths:** trigonometry; puzzles involving navigation **Science:** stars
1851	Birth of Martinus Beijerinck, microbiologist and botanist	**Science:** microbiology; botany
1859	Birth of Alexander Popov, physicist	**Science/Technology:** practical applications of radio waves
1912	Lawrence Oates leaves Scott's expedition to go off and die	**Science:** hypothermia; vitamins (poor diet was a possible factor in expedition failure)
1935	Death of John McCleod, biochemist and physiologist, Nobel laureate	**Science:** hormones, especially insulin
1958	The Ford Motor Company produced its 50 millionth automobile	**Maths:** appreciation of number; percentage increase in cars since 1958 **Technology/Engineering:** car design **Science:** pollution issues
1962	Birth of Philippe Kahn, technology innovator and enterpreneur	**Technology/Engineering:** design of mobile phones; design of phone cameras
1966	Launch of Gemini 8, 12th manned American space flight and first space docking	**Food technology:** what do astronauts eat? **Technology/Engineering:** factors involved in successful docking **Science:** space; gravity; rockets; forces **Maths:** speed calculations
1978	Supertanker Amoco Cadiz splits in two after running aground, resulting in the fifth largest oil spill in history	**Science:** pollution; oil **Technology/Engineering:** tanker design **Science/Technology:** cleaning up oil spills; opportunity to do practical work **Maths:** costs involved; area of oil spill
1998	Death of Derek Barton, chemist and Nobel laureate	**Science:** organic chemistry

Note: only about one-quarter of the STEM-related events are shown for this day. Most events could be modified for use across a wide age range.

Handling historical objects can be very emotive. A study involving 1,324 students, aged 5–18 years, from 40 schools, carried out by The Museum Network (2008–2009) showed that 82 per cent of students preferred learning using real objects, compared to 18 per cent who preferred using images. The study also suggested that real objects have a significant impact on learning and motivation, with students who had handled objects having more positive responses to questions about what they had achieved compared to those working

Table 2.4 Examples of STEM topics stimulated by the use of objects

Object	Possible STEM topic/s
Gas mask	Gases; oxygen transport in blood
Mink collar	Invasive species; intensive farming; insulation; materials
Slide rule	Calculations; design
Bakelite radio	Sound waves; materials; plastics; polymers; design

with images. Sixty-five per cent of those who handled objects wanted to find out more, compared with 50 per cent of those who had not handled objects.

Examination of objects can provoke many questions:

- What is it?
- What is it made of?
- How was it used?
- How has it been preserved?
- What do we use instead today and why?

Searching for answers can lead to further questions and provide context for topics under study. Handling objects can also develop observation, drawing, communication and data collection skills.

If it is possible to provide a collection of the same type of object, but made at different times (stethoscopes, calculators or printed circuit boards, for example) there is then added potential to demonstrate progression and discuss social, cultural, historical, ethnographic and scientific contexts.

Another approach comes from the Education and Outreach Committee of the British Society for the History of Science (2011), with their 'object autobiographies' project. This is not a new idea: Brough (1859) wrote as a carbon atom and Gibson (1911) wrote *The Autobiography of an Electron*. Creative writing can help students consider different perspectives and develop powers of empathy. If they are encouraged to write a story from the viewpoint of the object, this develops communication and literacy skills and encourages imagination. The British Society for the History of Science (2011) website gives a link to a pdf with examples of object stories, including that of an artificial leg!

What sort of objects? Almost anything that students may not be familiar with can act as stimulus material. Your History colleagues may be able to provide ideas if you tell them the topic. Some examples of objects that could be used are given in Table 2.4.

Where to find objects? Explore the recesses of cupboards in classrooms, labs and prep rooms. Circulate a request to other staff. Search charity shops and car boot sales. Old objects do require care to ensure that they are safe for pupils to touch, e.g. they may need cleaning or checking for splinters. Some items should not be handled at all, e.g. some older stuffed animals contain arsenic.

If nothing comes to light, museum loans may be the way forward. Many museums provide boxes of artefacts to loan to schools, often for little charge apart from carriage costs. The usual expectation is that the contents will be handled, so objects are usually duplicates or less precious items. Even so, students should handle them with respect.

Drama

There are some great resources for teaching STEM subjects through drama for younger students. For example:

- Dramatic mathematics (Back and Lee 2003)
- Teaching engineering using dramatic play (DeRusha and Wolfson 2010)
- *Dramatic Science: Using Drama to Inspire Science Teaching for Ages 5 to 8* (McGregor and Precious 2013).

There is growing interest in using drama to teach STEM subjects to students of all ages. Students could research, write and act their own plays. This might take more than one lesson and offers opportunities to involve other departments. The research and writing could be completed collaboratively and the performance could be during a second lesson.

Alternatives include:

- Students act out a play from a provided script.

  Example: *Performing Science* (Abrahams *et al.* 2011) has scripts and lesson plans for topics usually covered by 11–16-year-olds in Biology, Chemistry and Physics. A section helps teachers to design their own drama and role-play activities.

- Actors come into school to present a play.

  Example: the Biochemical Society, working in collaboration with the Islington Community Theatre in London, has produced three drama projects since 2009 around 'hard to teach' biomolecular topics 'with the aim of communicating the Science and encouraging discussion . . . on the associated issues'. One of these plays, Hive 9, about evolution, is performed in a lab, which adds impact.

A particularly interesting chapter in *Performing Science* includes evidence-based arguments about the value of using drama in Science. These could be applied to all STEM subjects and this chapter is highly recommended reading.

Culture

Widening the examples of STEM people mentioned in lessons, to go beyond 'dead, white, European males', can help to raise appreciation of the influence and contributions of other cultures on current knowledge and understanding. This can include inventions, processes and ideas, many of which came from beyond the Western world. In a multiethnic classroom, there may be students proud to have their country recognised and who may be able to contribute additional information.

The Science Programme of Study for 11–14-year-olds suggests that students 'trace the development of science worldwide and recognise its cultural significance'.

Students should also have a cultural understanding: 'Recognising that modern science has its roots in many different societies and cultures, and draws on a variety of valid approaches to scientific practice' (National Curriculum 2008, under review: Science).

Examples of opportunities for cultural inclusion and diversity

- Arithmetic, Algebra and Geometry: refer to *The Nine Chapters on the Mathematical Art*, the most important work on the history of Mathematics in China, based on first-century ideas, and the oldest Maths book in existence (Kangshen *et al.* 2000).
- Atomic structure: include the impact of Greek and Arabic ideas on the development of theories about atoms.
- Circulatory system: mention Charles Drew, the African-American who founded blood banks.
- Electricity/Electrical Engineering: teach about different conventions for mains circuits around the world.

- Metals/Materials Technology: mention ideas of the alchemists, including Muslim and European scholars.
- Nutrition/Food Technology: use diverse sets of non-European foods for carrying out food tests; compare diets in different cultures.

Making use of local and national cultural diversity can also add relevance to lessons. If any famous scientists, technologists, engineers or mathematicians lived or worked in your locality, make use of them. Find out if an important discovery was made in your region or whether there are sites of industrial importance or institutions with STEM links close by.

Useful resources

- *Teaching Science to Every Child: Using Culture As a Starting Point* (Settlage and Southerland 2012).
- The British Society for the History of Science Travel Guide to Scientific Sites, a website for anyone interested in finding out about places with links to the history of Science, Technology and Medicine around the world.
- A tea towel! Produced by Scienceshirts and available via their website, the tea towel shows British pioneers of Science linked to UK locations. Some of the 'scientists' featured are also technologists, engineers and mathematicians.
- Local museums and libraries.

Practical work

An agreed definition of what is meant by 'practical work' is not easy to find. The National Strategies (2008) defined it, for Science, as: 'Any activity that enables pupils to have direct, often hands-on, experience of the phenomena they are studying.'

For STEM subjects, this might be extended to include one or more of the following types of 'practical' work, which is still not exhaustive and has some overlapping categories.

Research	Projects or investigations	Modelling
Observations	Fieldwork	Role play
Pilots/trials	Data collection	Evaluation
Methods: following, testing or creating recipes/instructions	Data analysis – primary or secondary	Discussion
Designing	Making	Debate
Surveys	Computer simulations	Further research

Whatever type of 'practical' is carried out, what matters is its effectiveness and that students enjoy and learn from the activity. Some students have the skill of looking busy but learning little.

In an evaluation of the Getting Practical: Improving Practical Work in Science project, which aimed to improve the effectiveness of practical work in all schools in England by providing professional development training for teachers, the following conclusions were drawn:

- Primary and secondary schools use structured 'recipe'-style tasks, resulting in highly efficient practical work, enabling students to do what the teacher intended.
- No lesson plans included *explicit* strategies for helping students to link findings to scientific ideas. This meant that students were less able to use theory to interpret results and to evaluate their data.

As a result of these findings, it was suggested that teachers could make practical work more effective by integrating both a 'hands-on' and 'minds-on' approach, perhaps by including specific strategies when planning practical work (Abrahams and Reiss 2012).

Being 'engaged in practical work' is a factor that students claim makes lessons inspirational (Wilson and Mant 2011). Although allowing space and time for creativity may generate true innovation, such 'free-range' practical work is probably best relegated to non-lesson time. Lesson time is usually so precious that practical work generally needs a clear focus. The focus might be one or more of:

- developing knowledge and understanding
- learning practical skills
- developing an understanding of problem-solving learning.

It has been argued that students learn best by getting things wrong (Price-Mitchell 2011). This does not mean endorsing guessing, but encouraging students to absorb setbacks and to use them constructively to move forwards.

Students initially tend to dislike not getting the 'right' answer but supporting students to trial practicals, construct prototypes and to build and explore models should get them past expecting to follow a recipe to get to an already known answer. Developing the confidence to correct errors and then do things differently has the potential to motivate students, enhance creativity, encourage independence and promote learning.

This section ends with two examples of successful lesson-based practicals. Note the frequency of the 'E buzzwords'.

Science: Biology

Who? 16–17-year-olds, studying Human Biology

What? Walking in pink paint to create footprints to compare with photographs of fossil footprints of early hominids

Why successful?

It was a risky activity (possibility of mess) and so felt exciting

Never been done before; students felt trusted by teacher to explore new methods

Teacher got respect from the class for letting them do something unusual

Class totally engaged and hugely interested in the (unknown) outcome

Novelty aspect; students not used to undressing, even though only feet, in Science

Clear relevance to topic under study; linking practical to theory

Careful planning ensured health and safety issues addressed

Further details

Clarke *et al.* (2012)

Food Technology

Who? Students, 3–18 years

What? World Food Day

Why successful?

Using music helped students think about other cultures

Debating 'big questions', e.g. meat consumption, allowed discussion and exploration of the topic

Live 'tweetups' on solving global hunger allowed students to question experts

'Missions' challenged students to think creatively and critically about food sources

Planning and cooking a 'sustainable' meal brought theory and practice together

Most students enjoyed experiencing new foods

Further details

From the 'How to Teach' series, Guardian online teacher network. This example comes from How to teach . . . World Food Day (Drabble 2012b). Others in the series include: How to teach . . . astronomy, gravity, polar meltdown, mini-beasts, World Health Day, drought, winter solstice, National Tree Week, saving energy and children to cook (Drabble 2011a–c, 2012 a–f, 2013).

Effective use of information and communications technology (ICT)

Students know about an ever-increasing variety of ICT. Instead of banning mobile phones, as some schools do, these and other technological gadgets could be used, as other schools do, to find new ways of engaging students and making the curriculum relevant.

Some of the hardware and software that could be usefully used in STEM lessons includes:

Dataloggers   Digital cameras and microscopes

iPads, e-readers, tablets, etc.   iPods, iTunes U, MP3 players

Mobile/smart phones   Qwizdom (or similar audience response kits)

Skype   Twitter

The variety of technology available for learning and teaching is likely to continue to grow. Case Study 2.1 illustrates one example of how relatively new technology can be used with great effect and Case Study 2.2 describes how students can use ICT to interview scientists.

CASE STUDY 2.1   Organelle wars using Twitter

Anne Osterrieder's (2012) and Robin Heyden's (2012) blogs tell the story of the cell organelle 'wars', a campaign by cell organelles to become 'President' that went 'viral'. The initial project involved creating campaign posters with an 'election day' where students take on the role of organelles and give speeches about why they are the most important organelle, followed by voting. This is good learning and teaching, but not that unusual. The unusual twist was Brad Graba (@Mr_Graba) encouraging his Illinois Biology class to open Twitter accounts in the names of their organelles and to start posting messages.

Some messages, limited by Twitter to 140 characters, were witty:

> Cell membrane: 'PROTECTOR OF CELL CITY! VOTE FOR CELL MEMBRANE, WE KEEP THEM BAD GUYS OUT!'

> Nucleus: 'The data of everything about you inside of us. Vote for someone who knows you better than yourself.'

> Mitochondrion: 'With great power, comes great responsibility.'

In less than a day, some cell biologists noticed the Tweets. One, Anne Osterrieder, of Oxford Brookes University, UK, re-tweeted and blogged about the project. She also helped the students by suggesting the use of 'Storify' (storify.com) to help assemble their Twitter stream, images and resources. Other scientists joined in, to the delight of the class and teacher, as Anne explains:

> Mr Graba emailed me this morning to say how stunned his students were that real scientists followed and interacted with them: 'I cannot tell you how excited my kids and I are about having scientists from as far away as England and France getting involved in our little classroom project!'

> (Osterrieder 2012)

Scientists added to the Twitter stream, giving students more information. Some even asked to vote! The BBC became involved when John Runions (@JohnRunions), 'Dr Molecule' on BBC Radio Oxford, found out about the project and suggested that the students used the hashtag '#organellewars'. Having a hashtag makes it easier to find posts.

Why was this so successful for the students?

- Students used new technology to enrich their studies.
- The teacher structured the project so students understood what to do and how to do it.
- The students were given choices, of organelles and posts.
- Feedback and exchange with scientists and the BBC showed the students that others valued and were enthusiastic about their project.
- It was exciting for the students to get Tweets, almost daily, from practising scientists.
- Students gained enhanced understanding of the topic and how scientists work.
- The teacher enjoyed external responses to his class's project.
- It was exciting for scientists to encourage the students and follow the 'election campaign'.

Chapter 9 has lists of some useful Twitter 'handles' – people and organisations useful to 'follow' for STEM information.

CASE STUDY 2.2   I'm a scientist, get me out of here!

This online event allows students to interact with scientists via an 'X Factor' type of competition between participating scientists. Students act as judges.

Scientists try to answer questions submitted by students. Students then have live online conversations with the scientists, where they:

- ask questions
- learn more about the scientists
- let scientists know their opinions.

These events run in March, June and November. More information is available from the 'I'm a Scientist' website.

There are many more exciting examples of how ICT is being used to enhance STEM lessons, including using Skype to interview industrialists and mathematicians. To get started, make use of online tutorials, make friends with your IT technicians and find out what your students already know and can do.

STEM ambassadors and other visitors

Most students find it exciting to have outside visitors. With forward planning, it is possible to use a visitor to help enliven and contextualise most topics. STEM ambassadors all have a STEM background and training about what schools expect. They come with areas of expertise and may be prepared to be more interactive than just talking, perhaps demonstrating an idea or providing an insight into how a subject studied at school is used in industry. Contact your local STEMNET coordinator to let him or her know what type of expertise you are looking for. Chapter 5 discusses STEM ambassadors working with STEM clubs, but it is perfectly possible to involve ambassadors in lessons.

Speakers can also be found from speaker databases. Box 2.1 describes some of these.

Box 2.1   Speaker databases

There are various speaker databases. Some work with filters that allow searching by topic, age group or postcode.

Biology4All Speakers database

This subject-specific speaker database is hosted by the Biology4All website and is sponsored by the Biochemical Society. It lists university staff who will visit schools and speak on their specialism. Most do not charge; some ask only for travel expenses and others will not even ask for these, if it is part of their remit to do 'outreach' work or if sponsored by an organisation. In January 2013, over 545 separate talks were listed, including: 'How to poison your teacher and get away with it.'

(continued)

Box 2.1 (*continued*)

Sciencelive

An online directory of speakers, presenters and workshops delivered by professional Science and Engineering communicators and 'committed enthusiasts'. Coordinated by the British Science Association, supported by the Institute of Physics and funded by the Scottish government, it aims to make it easy to arrange visits across the UK.

Speakers for Schools

A speaker database, catering for all the STEM subjects. Created to provide students at state schools with the same access to inspirational speakers as those at fee-paying schools and for free. In January 2013 there were 800 speakers and 1,500 schools registered, with news of further funding to allow the programme to expand.

Once you have booked a speaker, make the visit as meaningful as possible by good communication beforehand. Make sure you know what the speaker can offer and that the individual is briefed about the class, to limit misunderstandings such as delivery at the wrong level. The website 'Windows to the Universe' has a 'Scientists in Schools' section on how to make classroom visits as productive as possible, including a checklist to give to visitors.

To help ensure a great lesson, suggest that speakers bring props. Anything not normally seen in school is usually interesting to students, though you may need to check that items are appropriate for school. One visitor to a lesson on classification brought along live snakes. It was a hot day, and the students could feel that the 'cold-blooded' boa constrictor was definitely not cold, something not intuitively understood from books or video clips. In fact, the boa was a bit too hot and demonstrated this by being sick on the front bench – a truly memorable lesson.

CREST Awards

Box 2.2 has information about CREST Awards, for ages 11–19 years. CREST Star Awards are also worth using with students, usually up to the age of 11. Some of the awards could be achieved in lessons. The CREST bronze award, for example, requires 10 hours of work. Spread across a few lessons and including students' own research and perhaps homework, award-level work could be reached without disrupting lessons. If topics are chosen carefully, then curriculum material could be extended and enhanced via working towards an award.

The British Science Association has some inspirational STEM case studies on its website to help with choosing projects.

Box 2.2   CREST Awards

History: Launched 1986–1987. CREST originally stood for CREativity in Science and Technology, but now that Engineering and Maths are included, CREST is just used as a name. CREST Awards have many curriculum links and are a creative way to engage with STEM.

Age range: 11–19 years.

Audience: Activities designed for lessons, clubs and beyond school, including work experience placements and individual projects.

Activities: A variety of projects from any STEM area, via students' own ideas or linked into existing industrial or academic research. Projects can be carried out in a variety of formats, including:

A British Science Association programme

- practical investigations, e.g. in Science
- making products, e.g. in Technology
- taking part in challenges, e.g. in Engineering
- analyses of data, e.g. in Maths
- designing a project, e.g. in Science communication
- researching, e.g. any STEM subject

or combinations of the above.

Managing the activities: Each Award has frameworks for students and teachers.

Uptake: Britain's largest national award scheme for STEM projects. In 2012, over 30,000 CREST Awards were undertaken.

Aims: To link 'personal passions of students to curriculum-based learning' and reward creative problem-solving.

CREST Award	Bronze	Silver	Gold
Usual age range (years)	11–14	14–16	16–19
Approx. length of project (hours)	10 Could be done as 'CREST in a Day'	30	70+
Focus	Fun, teamwork and transferable skills	Stretch and enrichment of studies	Real research
Project selection by	Students, teacher, local company or university, CREST link scheme, using the CREST online project ideas		

(continued)

Box 2.2 (continued)

CREST Award	Bronze	Silver	Gold
Relevance to curriculum and other activities	STEM links May be used to assess students before they start their 14–16 studies May suit students of varying ages with special educational needs or disabilities	STEM and coursework links Links with summer schools at higher education institutions Links with work experience and enterprise activities	Links with post-16 STEM studies Links with Nuffield Research Placements Links with work experience
	Useful STEM club activities		
	Helps with participation in events like National Science and Engineering Week (a week of projects could result in bronze or silver awards)		
Project approval	Teacher Mentor optional	Teacher Mentor, from higher education or industry optional but advisable	CREST local coordinator from higher education or industry required
Registration per student (£: as at Jan 2013)	4	8	15
Assessment. Awards can be completed by teams but assessment is individual	Internal, by another teacher	External: usually the local coordinator or project mentor	
	During assessment, students may present their work to the local coordinator/project mentor, by producing a poster or giving a talk. They may be encouraged to go on to present at regional or national fairs		

Links: CREST Awards may be regarded as the older sibling of the CREST Star Awards. CREST Awards have links to other schemes that use CREST for accreditation, such as:

- Global CREST Challenge – run by Practical Action
- Rotary Technology Tournaments – run by local Rotary Clubs
- Go4SET – run by the Engineering Development Trust.

Further information

- The British Science Association has lots of information on its Download Hub webpage, such as useful forms, free resources and guides to CREST, CREST Star and other schemes all in one place.
- The Universities and Colleges Admissions Service (UCAS) endorses CREST Awards for inclusion in students' personal statements.
- The CREST website has lots of ideas for projects, including a project resources section called 'Pick Up & Run', with ideas to help get started. This includes PowerPoint introductions for each level of CREST Award and more project ideas. Ideas can be downloaded as pdf documents. Topics cover: detective work, entertainment, fashion, food & drink, health and hygiene, life at the edge, space, sport and transport.
- Contact details for Coordinators are provided on the CREST pages of the British Science Association website. Coordinators can provide information on funding, sponsorship and CREST regional and national events.

Chapter 3

STEM outside the classroom and beyond the school gate

By the end of this chapter, you will have ideas about how to:

- provide opportunities beyond the classroom for students
- engage with opportunities to take part in National Science and Engineering Week, competitions, fairs and festivals
- find opportunities for STEM-specific professional development.

BEYOND THE CLASSROOM

Some opportunities for successful STEM sessions beyond the classroom are covered in other chapters; for example, Chapters 4 and 5 cover STEM clubs.

Learning outside the classroom adds value to students' learning and understanding, probably because it:

> provides a context for accumulating integrated and subject based knowledge and for developing key skills. Effective learning outside the classroom relies on problem-solving skills, cooperation and interpersonal communication: all essential skills for today's young people.
>
> (Council for Learning Outside the Classroom 2013a)

The National Centre for Excellence in the Teaching of Mathematics (2013) endorses this with the following statement on its website:

> Getting out of the classroom facilitates authentic or experiential learning . . . Pupils not only experience mathematics in concrete and novel settings, but can be liberated from the sometimes restrictive expectations of the classroom. As a result, we can expect to find the following benefits:
>
> - higher levels of motivation
> - almost limitless resources
> - an opportunity to see maths as cross-curricular
> - greater curiosity leading to more effective exploration
> - creative ideas driving investigations
> - meaningful application of problem-solving strategies and thinking skills
> - a heightened sense of purpose and relevance
> - the all-important bridge between theory and reality

- greater independence and an improved attitude to learning
- greater enjoyment and achievement (one of the five Every Child Matters outcomes)
- a realisation that our environment offers opportunities for learning and enjoyment.

These statements are based on studies such as:

1 The Programme for International Student Assessment in Focus study (2012). This suggested that students from schools offering more extracurricular activities:

   (a) had more positive attitudes towards the subject
   (b) believed in their own ability more
   (c) enjoyed learning Science more.

2 'Learning outside the classroom, how far should you go?' (Ofsted 2008). The impact of learning outside the classroom was evaluated in 12 primary schools, ten secondary schools, one special school, one pupil referral unit and three colleges across England. Improved outcomes for students were found, including 'better achievement, standards, motivation, personal development and behaviour'. Positive effects were also found on students normally hard to motivate.

3 The Royal Horticultural Society commissioned an evaluation of the impact of school gardening on students' learning and behaviour. The results suggested that taking part in gardening activities 'boosts child development, teaches life skills and makes kids healthier and happier' (Passy *et al.* 2010).

Using the school grounds

School grounds are valuable areas for enriching STEM subjects. Even schools in built-up areas with little green space have walls that can be investigated for lichens, kerbstones of possible geological interest or lightning rods for examples of conduction. Ponds can be created if there are none in the school grounds, by using containers (Howarth and Slingsby 2006).

Opportunities for STEM work in school grounds are almost endless. An activity such as mapping the biodiversity of school grounds could include:

- Science (identification of organisms)
- Maths (using scale)
- Design & Technology (designing and drawing maps).

Engineering might also be included if new structures such as greenhouses are considered. Table 3.1 gives further examples; more ideas can be found via Council for Learning Outside the Classroom (2013b).

Using areas of the school other than the school grounds

There are many areas of schools with potential for use within STEM lessons. Their lack of use may be considered a neglected resource. No one wants hordes of students trekking across busy parts of the school or appearing in rooms unexpectedly, but advance collaboration with colleagues should reduce 'nuisance' aspects.

Table 3.1 Some STEM uses of school grounds. Most of these activities can be adapted for ages 5–18

STEM subjects	Using school grounds
Biology	Ecological studies
	Walking with woodlice (Natural History Museum 2004, still accessible)
	Exercise and heart rate
	Further ideas: (97!) for 10–15-year-olds from OBIS, outdoor Biology website
Chemistry	Testing pH of soils and ponds
	Rock trail: identifying stones used in kerbs, lintels, rockeries and walls
	Metal trail: searching for uses of metals, corrosion and galvanisation
	Pollution studies: leaving sticky 'traps' or taking swabs
	Further ideas: Borrows (2006)
Physics	Sports areas for firing rockets and measuring distance travelled (Institute of Physics rocket kit is particularly good for this)
	Modelling interplanetary distances
	Coke and Mentos pressure demonstration (Howarth and Woollhead 2008)
	Further ideas: Outdoor Physics website, a bank of Physics ideas that uses the outdoors as a resource for teaching Physics
Technology	Designing, building and cooking with solar ovens
	Materials trail
	Observing structural design of different buildings
	'Grow and Cook' activities
	Further ideas: 'Learning Outside' DATA website
Engineering	Assembling/disassembling car engines
	Testing and trialling any large models
	Civil engineering trail: gates, arches, walls, etc.
	Further ideas: education webpages of the Royal Academy of Engineering
Maths	Shape treasure hunt
	Angles: using clinometers to measure heights of trees
	Circumference and area: using chalk to draw puddles as they evaporate
	Further ideas: from the Outdoor Maths website

Assuming classrooms, labs, workrooms and computer rooms are normally used for STEM teaching, where else, apart from the school grounds, can students learn about STEM? Table 3.2 has suggestions.

Beyond the school gates

Some research about the benefits of learning outside the classroom has already been described. Other research, more specifically about trips beyond the school gates, suggests that trips can have powerful enhancement and enrichment effects, such as:

- being remembered long after a visit (Falk and Dierking 1997)
- influencing career choice (Salmi 2003)
- increasing interest and engagement in science regardless of prior interest in a topic (Bonderup Dohn 2011).

Table 3.2 Different areas of the school that could be used for learning and teaching about STEM

School area	Suggested STEM purposes
Sports hall	**Science** • Area for particle role play • Height for experimenting with balloons with different gas contents **STEM** • Model parachutes, if balcony or climbing frame available • Poster displays or exhibitions of work • *In situ* studies of properties and performance of different polymers and technical fabrics, e.g. different sports balls, sports wear
School hall or room with a stage	**STEM** • Plays by students or presented to students • Presentations created by students • Shows by invited presenters
Food technology rooms	**Science** • Practicals involving food, e.g. constructing DNA models with sweets; making ice-cream using salt to freeze the mixture and creating 'chocolate rock cycles'; consumption could then be allowed on successful completion **Maths** • Recipes: practising weighing and measuring; calculating scaled up/down recipes • Celebrating Pi Day, 14 March, with a pie lesson, including calculating angles for different numbers of slices
School canteen	**Design & Technology** • Plan a menu for school students to be served from the school canteen. Advice from the canteen supervisor would help set the context and provide information about costs, preparation and cooking time, equipment and staff available
Art room	**STEM** • Drawing, painting, modelling, artefacts linked to topic; planets would be great to illustrate this way
History room	**STEM** • Stimulating for any historical aspects of STEM subjects. See section on using History earlier in the chapter
Whole school	**STEM** • Monitoring and evaluation of energy use throughout the school • Surveys such as effectiveness of recycling • Working towards the Green Flag Eco-schools programme
Ask the students	**STEM** • Ask students to take you to their favourite classrooms and explain what they like about them. Use this to make a positive change in your usual teaching room

Table 3.3 Strategies to help make trips and visits happen

Possible issues	Strategies to combat issues
Staff absence may affect classes	Advance planning can reduce issues
	Including school technicians may improve staff/ student ratio
Cost for students	Chapter 8 discusses funding
Cost for schools, including staff cover	Find out if the school has a budget to help with this
	Prepare strong arguments for value of the trip by addressing departmental and whole school aims
Risk assessments to be written or updated	Chapter 7 gives advice about risk assessments
Advance research, form filling, communication with other staff and parents	Most schools have visit checklists to help and proformas for letters and permission forms
Clash with other trips or sporting fixtures	Forward planning; getting your trip into the school calendar is essential
May disappoint due to adverse weather or quality of experience	A teacher preview visit is advisable; many venues allow this at no cost

With such benefits, it is no surprise that many teachers acknowledge the value of trips for generating interest and exposing students to new experiences (Kisiel 2005). The current government is keen for all teachers to be able to 'prepare or take part in activities, such as leading or taking part in Science field trips . . . this includes planning activities and trips to consolidate and extend the knowledge and understanding pupils have acquired' (House of Commons Report 2011a).

However, some teachers are wary about trips or managers are hesitant to endorse them. Some possible issues linked to trips are given in Table 3.3, along with suggestions for reducing concerns.

Trips can be divided into visits that involve working with the local community and other visits.

Working with the local community

Local projects

Getting involved in local projects really brings theory to life. Projects may involve a variety of STEM people and perspectives.

EXAMPLE

A unique university and community library, history and 'customer centre', the Hive, was built in Worcester in 2012. Biomass boilers and natural ventilation minimise environmental impact. Water from the River Severn is used to provide supplementary cooling. Local school students, aged 9–15, were involved in trialling the water flow cooling system by modelling the process. Discussions with engineers and environmental scientists helped inform their project. There is further scope to study the impact of the water removal and return on the ecology of the river in future.

Work experience

Work experience schemes, mainly for 16–19-year-olds, provide opportunities to get involved in STEM. Good STEM placements may influence choice of university course and/or ultimate career. If not available during school time, then students could be encouraged to use holidays for useful work experience.

Personal links with local institutions can help with finding relevant work experience. STEM fairs or events where industries and other employers are likely to be present may also be helpful in finding placements. The National STEM Centre e-library also has a section on finding quality STEM work experiences.

Other visits

With most school departments limited in numbers of trips allowed, it is important to choose visits carefully for maximum impact. An overview of visits across the years should help ensure all students get access to a range of visits. Table 3.4 suggests some useful STEM venues, and Case Study 3.1 describes a STEM visit to a university.

CASE STUDY 3.1   Visit of school students to Newcastle University

Students from a school in Stockton-On-Tees visited Newcastle University to take part in a 'flood conference and workshop'. They worked with undergraduates, lecturers and local people who had experienced flooding to test equipment that measured water levels and to discuss measures to prevent future flooding.

The students had access to statistics that allowed them to study current flood risks across the North-East of England. This led to drawing a map and developing an action plan for their local area, focused on the Rivers Tees and Yarm.

Following the visit, the students continued to work with advisors met at the conference, to develop their project. Their work should help lead to their school being one that specialises in climate change.

Information from 'Cameron' via the STEM clubs network website.

Visits that might involve a residential stay are not included in Table 3.4. Residential visits can promote fuller STEM immersion by students and might include:

- Summer camps:
  o Carter (2013) describes an exemplar programme for a summer camp, non-residential, for 10–11-year-olds.
  o Salters' Chemistry Camps are residential camps for 15-year-old students to explore chemistry and be motivated into long-term interest in the subject. Summer 2012 saw 14 camps hosted at universities throughout the UK.
- Olympiads: Table 3.6 (see below) has further details of Olympiads and other competitions. These can become residential once students get through qualifying rounds.

Table 3.4 Suggestions for non-residential STEM visits (residential visits are discussed later)

Venue	Further information
Cinema Like theatre, cinema visits may be an underused resource	A film with STEM content, *Contagion*, is great for 17–18-year-olds studying infection and immunity. Now available on DVD or by streaming; worth watching out for new films
Field study centres One-day visits possible if distance is not too far. Useful introductions to ecology if school does not have its own equipment or experts	Centres run by the Field Studies Council provide expertise Other, privately run centres can be excellent
Industry Visits possible across all STEM subjects Car manufacturers (Hughes 2013b) and the BBC make good venues (see opposite) A venue such as Cadbury's World addresses many aspects, including engineering, technology processes, food technology	The BBC hosts events for students to discover the technical side of broadcasting, e.g. the BBC Women in Engineering initiative for young technologists for 14–16-year-olds
Masterclasses Often attended by students aged 12–14 years old, usually on a Saturday morning, so not strictly a school visit, but worth including. There are also Masterclasses for younger and older students	The Royal Institution has been holding Maths Masterclasses for over 30 years and Engineering Masterclasses for over 3 years
Museums, exploratories, nature reserves, botanic gardens, zoos Most museums, exploratories and zoos have education officers; some offer teaching sessions for schools, often with items to handle Most offer previsit information as well as activities to do during visits and sometimes follow-up activities	Guidance on enhancing student learning on museum visits: the Open University has a free resource 'enhancing pupil learning on museum visits', available via its 'Open Learn' education web pages (http://www.open.edu/openlearn/education/enhancing-pupil-learning-on-museum-visits/content-section-0) Using museum dioramas: Reiss and Tunnicliffe (2011) Primary visits to the zoo: Smith (2013)

(continued)

Table 3.4 (continued)

Venue	Further information
Research institutes Include: • Universities • Commercial research organisations, e.g. GSK • Large museums, such as the Natural History Museum in London	Nuffield Research Placements, carried out in students' summer holidays, are described in Box 5.2 in Chapter 5 Case Study 3.1 describes students visiting Newcastle University
STEM fairs, festivals and competitions A later section in this chapter has information about fairs, festivals and competitions For students and teachers that attend these, it is often a highlight of their year – see opposite	'@HRogerson said that her visit to the Big Bang Fair was the best trip ever; host @MrsDrSarah agrees stongly, having judged at the fair in the past' Tweet during scheduled ASE Chat, Topic 59, July 2012
Theatres An underused resource; lots of plays involve interesting STEM material Note: there are also bad plays about STEM subjects, so advance research recommended	Some plays with a STEM content to watch for: *A Disppearing Number*, Complicité Co. *Arcadia*, Stoppard *Copenhagen*, Frayn *Galileo Galilei*, Brecht *Proof*, Auburn *The Doctor's Dilemma*, Shaw *The Physicists*, Dürrenmatt
Theme parks Claimed to be useful for the Physics of rollercoasters; certainly looked forward to by students	Thorpe Park and Alton Towers are amongst the most popular in England M&Ds theme park in Scotland has a tropical rainforest

- Student conferences or forums, for example, the London International Youth Science Forum. Founded in 1959, this 2-week London-based event attracts around 350 Science students, aged 17–21, from over 50 countries each year.

Unfortunately, this, and other conferences, can be quite expensive. In 2013, it cost £1,495 to participate in the London IYS Forum.

- Taster programmes:
  - o Example 1: Headstart programmes: Established for over 16 years, 'home' students, aged 16–17 years old, are subsidised to attend STEM courses at universities, including broad-based engineering and more specialised courses. Further details from the EDT website, Headstart pages.
  - o Example 2: Smallpeice Trust Engineering Experiences: Subsidised courses (£0–475 in 2013) for 12–17-year-olds, based in universities and designed to show that engineering is exciting and varied. Further details from the Smallpeice website.
- Longer field trips: Often based in environmental or field study centres, students have opportunities to complete coursework projects or investigations, as well as travel to more interesting destinations than one-day visits allow.
- Trips abroad: There are wonderful opportunities for students and teachers to travel to amazing destinations to carry out STEM projects or visit internationally renowned institutions such as CERN in Switzerland. Some organisations offer sponsorship for major visits like these; the alternative is to plan ahead and fund-raise. Chapter 7 has advice about risk assessments; Chapter 8 has ideas for fund-raising.

Whenever trips or visits are undertaken, encourage students to take photographs and keep notes. On return, these could help with presenting to other members of the school and/or parents, so that:

- others are enthused to take part in the future
- participants evaluate and share their experiences
- the whole school can celebrate the venture.

A free resource, downloadable from the Windows to the Universe website, from the 'snapshot' page, helps younger students write about visits.

Referring to the learning described in the students' blogs and presentations, in a visit report to the school senior management and governors, will strengthen the arguments for the value of the trip and improve the chances of a repeat trip being authorised and perhaps even (part) funded in the future.

Taking part in National Science and Engineering Week, competitions, fairs and festivals

National Science and Engineering Week

National Science and Engineering Week (NSEW) is not a week, but 10 days, every March, of exciting events celebrating STEM across the UK. NSEW is coordinated by the British Science Association, in partnership with EngineeringUK, and has the Department for Business, Innovation and Skills (BIS) as a major sponsor.

NSEW events can be organised by anyone, but the 'week' provides schools with great opportunities to raise the profile of STEM for students. It is free to register as an NSEW event organiser. There is no commitment to run your event, but linking to NSEW has many advantages:

- raised school profile through listing in national NSEW programme
- increased publicity via NSEW marketing strategies
- use of NSEW yearly theme to act as a 'hook' for your events
- advice, activities, competitions and funding ideas.

Figure 3.1 shows some NSEW activities we have seen that work well. Whatever your event, remember to take photos and create displays. There are no rules about event formats, apart from having a STEM theme. Further information can be found on the NSEW pages of the British Science Association website.

Competitions

Whether winning or taking part, using competitions to enhance learning has numerous benefits. Participating students have chances to be creative and go beyond the curriculum.

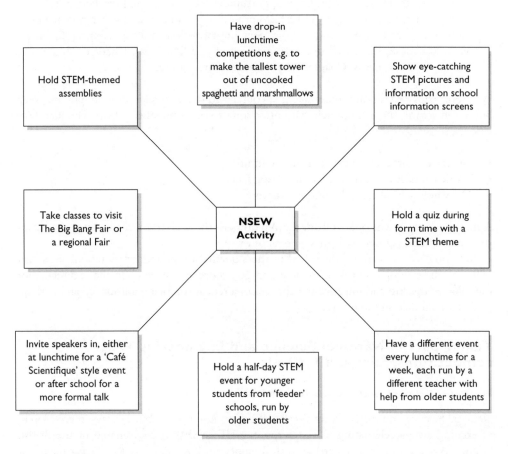

Figure 3.1 Ideas for National Science and Engineering Week (NSEW) activities in school, which could also be run at other times.

Competitions can provide opportunities to contact experts in industry and research. Students who go on to win or receive positive feedback get external endorsement of the value of their work. Competitions can provide teachers with wider choices for homework, as well as professional development if topics are outside their area of expertise. Success in organising competition entries may help towards promotion, perhaps as STEM coordinator.

For the school, competitions can provide rationales for running STEM clubs (see Chapter 4). Good publicity raises the school's profile and increases the status of STEM subjects, perhaps with positive effects on students' choices of further study at school and beyond. Handled well, competitions can turn school 'work' and home 'work' into something just as productive for learning, but more fun. However, be aware of potential issues with competitions. Table 3.5 addresses some of these in relation to STEM.

There are many exciting STEM competitions. Perhaps the difficult decision is choosing appropriate ones for your students. STEM coordinators have a key role here in encouraging staff to collaborate over planning so students are not overloaded. Table 3.6 outlines types of competitions. Whilst some competitions have been around a long time, others may be more ephemeral, so examples should be regarded as generic rather than specific. Any that disappear are likely to be replaced by others, so be vigilant for new competitions to use in class or with STEM clubs.

More examples of competitions are given in two articles in *School Science Review* (Scott and Howarth 2011; Howarth and Scott 2011b). Maintaining an overall view of your school's participation in STEM competitions helps continuity and building on successes. An annual plan, as shown in Table 3.7, may contribute to an overview. This could be further broken down into specific year groups.

Once the hard work is over, don't forget to celebrate participation and successes. Thank staff involved, provide management with an impact report and encourage participants to enthuse younger students to create continuity. Make good use of all the marketing tools at your disposal so that everyone knows about the wonderful STEM opportunities at your school. Also, remember to encourage staff to enter competitions as well as students (see the last section of this chapter).

Table 3.5 Some issues with competitions

Competitions	
Issues	*Solutions*
Failure may damage self-esteem	Provide prizes or award certificates of participation for worthy efforts
Difficulties of ensuring inclusion: some students may have more sophisticated software or tools or fabrics than others	Give the same materials to all students
	Create rules about what may/may not be used
Some students may be discouraged from trying if they perceive no chance of winning	Choose the appropriate level of challenge
	The National STEM Centre elibrary has good advice on the British Science Association STEM Projects Toolkits pages
Potential of stress	Emphasise activities rather than outcomes
	Working in teams may reduce individual anxiety
Not all students motivated or interested in competing	Offer choice
	Encourage participation, but make entering optional

Table 3.6 Examples of STEM competitions

Type of competition	Age range (years)	Examples	Comments
Careers	16–17	**Making Materials Matter** Organised by TATA Steel, the Institute of Materials, Minerals and Mining (IOM3) and the Armourers and Brasiers Company	Materials Science and Engineering is a career considered by few students. This competition aims to raise awareness of the discipline Details: IOM3 website
Communication	5–18	**Royal Society of Chemistry Bill Bryson Science Communicators Award** Designed to recognise and encourage excellent science communication; each year has a theme	Entries accepted in any format, e.g. videos, posters, cartoons, poems. Must communicate science accurately and appropriately for chosen audience Details: RSC website, education pages
Innovation	5–14	**Poster competition organised by the British Science Association** (BSA) Coincides with National Science and Engineering Week in the UK	Students design a product linked to the annual theme Details: BSA website, National Science and Engineering Week pages
Challenges	9–10	**Primary Mathematics Challenge** Run by the Mathematical Association for schools across the UK	Multiple-choice, interesting mathematical problems for top 60 per cent of students Details: Mathematical Association website
	11–14	**STEM Challenges** Ten archived activities, inspired by the Olympic Games 2012	Information and challenges available: BSA website on CREST Award pages
	13–14	**Biology Challenge** Encourages interest in Biology beyond the curriculum	Online questions, e.g. multiple choice, identification or matching Details: British Biology Olympiad website, Biology Challenge pages
Olympiads	17–19	**British Physics Olympiad** Challenges the best physicists in schools and selects the UK Physics Team	Exam-based. Individual entries until team selected Details: British Physics Olympiad website
Whole school, STEM-based	11–18	**National Science and Engineering Competition** Coordinated by the BSA in partnership with Young Engineers and The Big Bang The competition is split into (a) **Science and Maths** – discovery, exploration and explanation projects and (b) **Engineering and Technology** – design and manufacture projects	Students completing projects through schemes, e.g. CREST Awards or Young Engineer for Britain competition, can enter their project via regional Big Bang fairs or online self-nomination to compete for further prizes, including titles of UK Young Scientist of the Year and UK Young Engineer of the Year Details: The Big Bang Fair website

14–19	**Space Settlement Design Competition** Challenges students worldwide to tackle engineering briefs focusing on colonies in space Gives students glimpses of work pressures and priorities	Residential: Imperial College, London Teams design space settlements for up to 10,000 inhabitants, taking structural engineering, communications, entertainment, food production, construction timelines and cost into account. In 24 hours! Details: UK Space Design Competition website
Specific subjects		
Up to 11	**Young Mathematicians' Award** Organised by NRICH and Explore Learning	Teams compete at regional level. First rounds involve fun challenges. Final at the University of Cambridge Details: NRICH website, primary pages
11–14	**The Salters' Chemistry Club competitions** Makes Chemistry relevant and exciting	Word puzzles; answers on postcards. Great for homework. Class entries could be posted in one envelope Details: The Salters' Chemistry Club website
12–19	**Young Engineer for Britain** Encourages creative and innovative marketable projects	Individuals or teams can participate Participation in this competition can be found on many successful engineers' CVs Details: Young Engineer for Britain website
13–18	**Google Science Fair** This worldwide 'fair' is an online competition, challenging students to carry out scientific investigations	Students compete with peers in their age group Details: Google Science Fair website
Specific topics		
10+	**National Cipher Challenge** Online code-breaking competition, organised by Southampton University	Online codes to crack, independently or in teams Details: National Cipher Challenge website
14–17	**International Brain Bee** International neuroscience competition Motivates students to learn about the brain and consider careers in biomedicine	About 150 local coordinators in 30 countries conduct competitions annually Local winners attend their national competition. National winners compete in the International Championship. Details: International Brain Bee website

Table 3.7 Exemplar planner for STEM competition and award involvement

Age (years)	Term		
	Autumn	Spring	Summer
8–9	Maths games and challenges, preparing for Young Mathematicians' Award	Young Mathematicians Award CREST Star Awards	Royal Horticultural Society school gardens competition
10–11	'Kids school – eco learning' European project with Panasonic	National Science and Engineering Week (NSEW) Regional STEM club showcase	Project with older pupils to prepare for moving schools, e.g. CREST bronze
11–13	Junior Challenges, e.g. Maths	Rotary Club Design Technology competition	CREST bronze
14–16	CREST silver projects Formula1 Challenge	Biology, Chemistry, Maths, Physics Challenges Young Fashion Designer UK	Kangaroo Maths Challenge
16–19	CREST gold projects Nuffield Research Placements launch Outreach – supporting younger students	Biology, Chemistry, Maths, Physics Olympiads Young Engineer/Scientist competitions	Silverstone Design Challenge

For information about competitions see Table 3.6 or Chapter 9

STEM fairs and festivals

STEM fairs

Going to regional or national STEM fairs allows classes or clubs to show off what they have achieved and gain inspiration from seeing what others have done.

- The Big Bang Fair – the biggest single celebration of STEM in the UK. It shows students, 7–19 years old, the exciting and rewarding opportunities that exist for those with STEM experience and qualifications. Details of competitions and examples of projects are given in two articles (Howarth and Scott 2011a, 2012).
- The Big Bang Local and The Big Bang Near Me – regional fairs offering students opportunities to experience exciting hands-on learning outside the classroom and/or showcase their projects, without travelling long distances or overnight stays. Regional fairs can be gentle introductions to STEM competitions.
- Imagineering fairs give students opportunities to learn more about engineering in everyday life. Visitors can take part in hands-on activities and meet engineers.

STEM festivals

Edinburgh held the world's first Festival of Science and Technology in 1989 (Scottish Schools Education Research Centre 2013). Festivals range from subject-specific festivals for school students of particular ages to those open to anyone interested, on a 'drop-in' basis or by ticket. Unless you are going to hold your own school festival, not that uncommon in American schools, or encourage students to attend festivals during holidays, then travel to a venue may need to be considered.

Reasons to attend festivals need to be clear to obtain time out of school and the finance needed. There may be key speakers of national renown that make attendance worthwhile. Or there may be a programme of events, bookable in advance, so time is well spent and the visit can be justified.

Some examples of festivals are given in Table 3.8.

No festival is complete without buskers. If you are taking a class to a festival, make the most of every moment, such as eating lunch while watching impromptu events. The Maths Busking website is worth investigating.

STEM professional development

Embedding all those 'E' buzzwords, mentioned in the introduction to this chapter, into lessons requires enthusiastic and knowledgeable teaching. Students talk about their 'best' teacher as one who loves the subject and shares that passion through rich activities. Blatchford (2013) suggests that the heart of excellent progress by students, a current concern of most schools, is 'motivating and inspiring teaching'.

Table 3.8 Examples of STEM festivals

Festival	When	Where	Details
Salters' Festivals of Chemistry	1 day, March to mid-June	Universities around the UK and Ireland	Organised by the Salters' Institute and the Royal Society of Chemistry
			Teams of students, aged 11–12, carry out fun practicals, gain certificates and possibly prizes
British Science Festival	6 days in September	A different UK university city each year, e.g. 2014 is Birmingham	One of the UK's biggest Science festivals. Though Science is in its name, all STEM subjects are celebrated
Regional Science Festivals (two examples from 20 + in the UK)	14 days in March	Cambridge	University of Cambridge is both venue and coordinator. A range of programmes and activities is offered exclusively to schools, to enrich the curriculum and inspire pupils into the further study of Science
	6 days in June	Cheltenham	The Times Cheltenham Science Festival attracts 'big names' such as Brian Cox, Alice Roberts and David Attenborough. Packed with debates, experiments and hands-on learning
The North West Design and Technology Festival	March	Edge Hill University, Ormskirk, UK	For teachers of all age students, this celebrates outstanding practice in Design & Technology

Continuing professional development opportunities help maintain both breadth and depth of knowledge, along with passion and enthusiasm. Chapter 4 has examples of training available to help run STEM clubs. Table 3.9 gives other sources of professional development, specifically aimed at those teaching STEM subjects.

Table 3.9 STEM continuing professional development (CPD)

CPD source	Comment
Science Learning Centres	Cover all STEM subjects; many courses have bursaries that cover costs and possibly also supply cover
Subject professional bodies and associations	These offer many, usually free, local events around the UK; most subject organisations have strong online resources

Networking events	Examples:
	• Events coordinated by STEMNET contractors
	• 'Teachmeets' organised by the British Science Asssociation
	• Teacher networks, though for teachers of all subjects, can be customised to deliver STEM-specific materials. They include:
	
	   o Guardian online
	   o TES online forums
	   o Twitter (see Chapter 9)

Regional and national conferences	Example: the Association for Science Education annual conference
International conferences	Examples: • Geosciences Information For Teachers, subsidised conference in Vienna each spring • Comenius conferences, subsidised by the British Council; various venues
Summer schools	Examples: • The Science of Materials (Royal Society of Chemistry, Institute of Materials, Minerals and Mining (IOM3) and Armourers and Brasiers) annual residential summer school introduces Materials Science to Chemistry teachers of pre- and post-16 students • Science and Plants for Schools (SAPS), 4 days, for post-16 Biology teachers to learn from some of the world's leading researchers in Plant Science and develop new materials for their students (heartily endorsed by one of the authors) • Goldsmiths' Science for Society courses include Astronomy, Chemistry, Genetics, Materials Science, Mathematics, Particle Physics and Sustainable Energy. Two-week courses free for UK secondary teachers • Polymer Study Tours: 4-day residential courses free for 11–19-years teachers of Science and Design & Technology. Usually held in Edinburgh, London and Manchester in June/July

Masterclasses	Example: Materials Science organised by Rolls-Royce, Armourers and Brasiers and University of Birmingham. Residential. For teachers of Physics, Chemistry, Technology and general Science, pre- and post-16
Specific training	Examples: • Food Safety (DATA) • Plant Science (various Botanic Gardens and SAPS – see below)

Fellowships and Associates	Examples:
	• The NEF Industrial Fellowship scheme, from The Innovation Institute. Provides STEM FE lecturers with a grant to support secondment into industry (includes bioscience, construction, digital media, healthcare, ICT and manufacturing)
	• SAPS (Science and Plants for Schools) Associates Scheme. Free scheme for UK teachers, technicians and teaching associates, provides:
	  o grants
	  o teaching resources
	  o opportunities for professional development, including a summer school (see above)
	  o 'Ask the Experts' panel
	  o newsletters

Publications	Example: EiSXtra, an ASE member journal, has articles such as Helping STEM/Science Coordinators in Primary Schools (Hughes 2013)

Teacher competitions and awards

Having bought or borrowed this book, undertaken professional development by reading this far and perhaps implemented some of the suggested strategies, you are clearly a wonderful teacher and deserve an award. There are several awards, rewards and competitions open to STEM teachers in the UK. Some are subject-based, such as the Biology Secondary Teacher of the Year award, organised by the Society of Biology.

Primary colleagues may be honoured by one of the Primary Science Teacher of the Year awards, sponsored by AstraZeneca Science Teaching Trust. Traditionally there are six awards per year, one being for teaching under difficult circumstances.

Other awards include the general Teaching Awards, such as those sponsored by Pearson, with winners, often STEM teachers, featured on television. SATRO, an independent, not-for-profit social enterprise that exists to inspire young people about their future careers, organises a STEM Teacher of the Year award.

Some 'rewards' are career-orientated, such as opportunities to apply for STEM coordinator posts, of which there are a growing number in schools. There are also opportunities to make use of your expertise and experiences in competitions such as the Wellcome Trust Science Writing Prize.

Chapter 4

Starting and running a successful STEM club

By the end of this chapter, you will have an understanding of how to:

- start a STEM club
- run a STEM club successfully.

Starting a STEM club

The 2007 Review of Government's Science and Innovations Policies (Sainsbury 2007) recommended that all secondary schools had Science and Engineering clubs within 5 years. This was subject to detailed evaluation of a pilot club scheme and Chapter 1 covers some of the history behind this. The organisation STEMNET is managing this recommendation and its website gives considerable guidance for starting and running STEM clubs for all school-age students.

There are other websites that provide help to set up STEM clubs and it is worth spending time searching out ones that match your particular interests and age groups. Other sources of information include the regular articles in *School Science Review* that started in 2009 under the banner of 'The Clubbers' Guide' (e.g. Tosh and Short 2009).

From personal experience, having visited a range of secondary schools around the UK in the last few years, it is clear that there are still schools with no STEM clubs. Sometimes schools wrongly state that they have no STEM club, due to a misunderstanding that a club is only a 'STEM club' if it includes all the STEM subjects. However, single-focus clubs, such as a Robotics club or a Maths club, are considered to be STEM clubs. Traditionally, in England, STEM clubs, such as Science clubs, have been seen as a lunchtime or after-school activity. Increasingly though they are being used creatively to deliver curriculum enhancement activities (Chapman and Smith 2007).

Judging by the number of requests by teachers, on internet forums and elsewhere, help in setting up clubs is clearly needed. By the end of this chapter, we hope to convince you that setting up a club is not only possible, but one of the best things that you can do for your students, yourself, your school and possibly your community.

Overcoming barriers to setting up a club

Why don't all schools have a STEM club? Some common reasons are given in Table 4.1, with suggestions for solutions that could address most of these reasons. We hope that this will give you the confidence to make a start in setting up a club in your school.

Table 4.1 Reasons for not having a STEM club and solutions

Reason	Possible solutions
Lack of staff time	Make sure the Senior Leadership Team know the level of the government's encouragement for schools to have STEM clubs. Attempt to negotiate some staff time for planning and delivering. Cite evidence from recent Ofsted subject reports about the positive impact of engagement with enrichment activities
	Many schools in the UK have STEM coordinators. If your school doesn't, suggest the need for this role, with recognition in terms of time or money
	Involve many staff if possible, so one person does not do everything. If one keen person gets promoted or leaves for another school (and such enthusiastic people are likely to move on quickly), then the club may cease. With many people involved, this is less likely
	Involve technicians in any practical clubs; they may be able to set up sessions in advance, even if not available after school. Some technicians are virtually STEM coordinators, helping plan and organise sessions (Carter 2012)
Lack of student time	Find out when other clubs, training and practices are on. Schedule the new club to avoid clashes
	Find out when exams and assessments are on. Avoid running the club just before or during these
	If students depend on buses, then after-school clubs may be tricky. Consider other times or arrange with parents to collect students afterwards
Lack of staff interest	Hold sessions that interest staff. Find out staff interests and use STEM ambassadors or external speakers they may want to meet
	Offer staff a ready-made audience for them to carry out a favourite activity
	Give participating staff credit when writing up sessions, e.g. on the school website
	Ask for only one commitment per year or per term; this may help to bring more people on board
	Make it clear that helping contributes towards professional development
Lack of student interest	Find out what students want to do. Start with those ideas. Forensic science, explosions and making things are often top of students' wish lists
	Offer clear outcomes, e.g. CREST Awards, certificates or presentations so that students see what they are working towards
	Publicise successes via posters, parents' evenings, newsletters, websites so the club starts to gain a high profile and students get recognition for achievements
	Have music, food and soft drinks to create a different atmosphere from the classroom
Lack of funding	The school may have a budget for STEM activities. Find out. If not, ask for one
	There may be a budget for running clubs. Find out and apply for some of this
	Ask Parents' Associations to help
	Investigate sources of funding
	Make do with little. Many projects require little funding to be successful
	Read Chapter 8

(continued)

Table 4.1 (continued)

Reason	Possible solutions
Lack of resources	Make do with little. Many projects require little in the way of materials. Make a little go a long way, perhaps by students working in teams
	Use scrap stores or community recycling shops
	Ask parents to donate materials
	Search STEM organisations for ideas for resources
	Read Chapter 9
Lack of expertise	Use 'ready-to-go' resources such as those produced by professional bodies and others
	Take part in training, e.g. the Royal Academy of Engineering has developed courses for teachers, delivered by Science Learning Centres in the UK, that enable teachers to run programming activities successfully
	Invite experts, such as STEM ambassadors, to help
	Involve other staff, older students or parents with expertise to help run some sessions
	Read Chapter 3 about professional development

Presenting a case for starting a club

Once you have decided that setting up a club is feasible, the next steps may be to present a case to the Head or Senior Leadership team. Before this, you may want to have some facts and figures at your fingertips, including information about finances and potential interest by students and staff. Figure 4.1 provides a possible set of steps to follow.

When presenting a case for setting up a new STEM club, you may want to use some of the following persuasive arguments, mostly gathered from STEM coordinators in schools. STEM clubs can:

- build confidence in students struggling with STEM
- provide extra outlets for students with aptitudes in STEM who are interested in furthering their learning
- enrich and extend the curriculum
- move forward the learning of students (Sutton Trust 2011)
- improve attainment in, and experiences of, STEM for students
- motivate staff to extend their subject knowledge
- improve collaboration between staff and between schools
- improve collaboration between schools and industry, higher education and professional bodies
- encourage pupils to enrol in STEM-based qualifications
- increase uptake of STEM subjects beyond school
- raise the school profile by STEM club members participating in competitions and fairs
- bring additional resources and funding into school
- encourage enterprise and the entrepreneurs of tomorrow.

Decisions to make

Figure 4.1 shows that setting up a STEM club involves decisions. Further decisions include:

- The remit of the club – will it address several STEM subjects or be more specific, such as a Zoology club?
- When will the club run?
- What age/ability of students may be involved?
- What rooms are wanted?

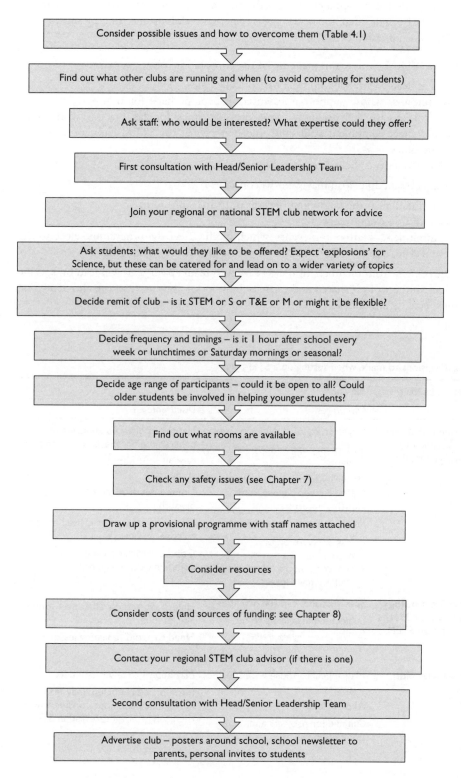

Consider possible issues and how to overcome them (Table 4.1)

Find out what other clubs are running and when (to avoid competing for students)

Ask staff: who would be interested? What expertise could they offer?

First consultation with Head/Senior Leadership Team

Join your regional or national STEM club network for advice

Ask students: what would they like to be offered? Expect 'explosions' for Science, but these can be catered for and lead on to a wider variety of topics

Decide remit of club – is it STEM or S or T&E or M or might it be flexible?

Decide frequency and timings – is it 1 hour after school every week or lunchtimes or Saturday mornings or seasonal?

Decide age range of participants – could it be open to all? Could older students be involved in helping younger students?

Find out what rooms are available

Check any safety issues (see Chapter 7)

Draw up a provisional programme with staff names attached

Consider resources

Consider costs (and sources of funding: see Chapter 8)

Contact your regional STEM club advisor (if there is one)

Second consultation with Head/Senior Leadership Team

Advertise club – posters around school, school newsletter to parents, personal invites to students

Figure 4.1 Possible timeline to follow when setting up a STEM club.

Table 4.2 suggests the advantages and disadvantages of options that you might choose. Once these have been decided, the next stage is to get your club up and running successfully. Further steps are suggested below.

1   Recruit a 'STEM clubs team' made up of the core staff involved, perhaps:
  • you as 'lead', with back-up via a rota of colleagues
  • technicians, whose support is essential, except perhaps for non-practical clubs. Technicians are likely to know about 'pressure times' for class practical work which could affect equipment availability and hence what the STEM club could offer at those times
  • older students to help or act as mentors.

2   Agree a club schedule. You may want to consider:
  • a start date near the beginning of term or further into term
  • gaps during exam weeks
  • commitment to attending events, which might affect the programme close to the event date, e.g. for a STEM clubs showcase at a local Big Bang Fair.

3   Get agreement from members of the STEM club team about who will lead on specific activities so the work is shared and capacity built in for continuity of the club if anyone is unexpectedly unavailable.

Table 4.2 Decisions to make when setting up a STEM club

(a) What will be the remit of the club?

Options	Advantages	Disadvantages
STEM club rather than Science, Technology, Engineering or Maths club	Huge variety of activities possible Variety may appeal to more students Flexibility to move on to new topics, linked to news items or students' interests Involvement of more staff, so: • less pressure on one department • reduced risk of club ceasing if a staff member leaves	Harder to draw up an inclusive programme if a specialist in one area Not all activities appeal to all students Limited depth at the expense of breadth Need several staff or invited experts to cover expertise Good coordination and communication required
Science, Technology, Engineering or Maths club rather than STEM club	Specialist staff can run activities Subject experts likely to be familiar with safety issues	Unless marketed well, it may sound like lessons Need to avoid repeating lesson content
Narrow-focus club Example: Textile club	May appeal to those with specific interests Allows depth Suitable for projects and competitions	May appeal to fewer students If the only STEM club, may lead non-participants into considering themselves not interested in STEM

Wide-focus club
Example:
A Sustainable Energy club could include monitoring energy consumption, building models, calorific analyses of different fuels, calculations and recycling projects

Suitable for cross-curricular work, so likely to involve several departments and staff, so a strong base for the club

Reduces the pressure on one department to run all the activities

Likely to appeal to many students due to potential variety of approaches

Good communication, coordination and collaboration between different staff and departments are vital

Some activities may not appeal to all students; students may drop out when emphasis shifts to areas of less interest

There may be limited depth to some activities if a 'scatter gun' approach is taken

(b) How long will club sessions be?

Options	Advantages	Disadvantages
30 min	Likely to fit into lunchtimes Might suit younger children Less time to get bored	Unless prompt start guaranteed, could reduce to 20–25 min Limited types of activity – but still lots possible
1–2 hours	Fits after-school models best Time to set up, carry out and clear away many activities	May feel similar to lessons Some activities may need longer or can only be partially completed in this time
2+ hours	Fits Saturday mornings or 'collapsed timetable' or holiday models best Offers chance to make real progress on a project or to have long sessions around themes	May need to be broken up into several shorter activities Time may need to be included for breaks, lunch Requires more staff time

(c) When will the club run?

Options	Advantages	Disadvantages
Lunchtime	Students on site Technicians around, but unless a staggered lunch break, may not be available or busy Plenty of people around so jobs could be shared out	Time may be too short to do much Staff, including technicians, and students need to eat lunch and set up for the afternoon Staff and students need a break
After school	Students on site Gives morning/afternoon to set up materials; technicians might help with this Easier for working parents and STEM ambassadors to attend and help	Students may need school bus to get home, so after school not possible Parents may not let students travel after dark, affecting November–December attendance in the UK Staff and students may be tired and have lesson preparation/marking/homework

(continued)

Table 4.2 (continued)

Options	Advantages	Disadvantages
	Less time-limited than lunchtime; more opportunities for lengthier activities	Lab and ICT technicians may not be employed beyond the end of the day
		Computer suites may be unavailable
		Need to ensure a named first aider is available on the premises
		Activities could be disrupted by cleaners
Saturday mornings/ afternoons	Less time-limited than after school	Saturdays are precious for staff and students for family time or hobbies
	Less time pressure, with no school work for staff or students to prepare for the following day	Sports teams often train or have fixtures; may prevent some students attending
	Parents, STEM ambassadors and other experts are more likely to be available	Care needed to make sure that all adults who turn up are invited and are DBS-checked and that only expected students attend
	Offers possibilities of using another site/students from different schools working together	Some areas of school not available outside normal school hours
	Could be run by a non-school organisation	Site needs to be known by at least one adult present
		First aider requirement, as above
		If run by a non-school organisation, can be expensive and exclude some students
Science weeks or blocks of time such as 'collapsed curriculum' days	Allows focus on a project without breaks in between	Could mean long periods when no extracurricular STEM activities occur
	Outcomes such as 'CREST in a day' possible	Long-term projects such as growing plants may not be possible
	More students may be involved as possibly fewer alternatives	Less opportunity for trial and error/ serendipitous outcomes
	Raised profile if several groups work towards common goals, e.g. presenting at a STEM fair	Extra staffing for 'mass participation' projects could mean unenthusiastic staff and poorer outcomes
	Allows advance planning; more likely to be 'one big effort'	May require many resources at the same time
Holidays	Many of the advantages for Science weeks apply	Some of the disadvantages for Science weeks apply
	Full days and longer themes possible	Staff and students need holidays
	More parents/staff from other schools might be available	Needs careful planning to ensure staff available
	Less restriction on start/end times makes trips easier	Issues of pay may arise for staff for additional holiday work
	During summer holidays, more opportunity to work outside	Areas of the school may not be available during holidays
		First aider requirement

	May be funding if some places reserved for students from targeted priority groups	
As and when needed/ wanted	Flexibility	Lack of continuity
	Ability to take part in new competitions or events	No regular programme may mean no regular core of students attending
	Could be 'high-profile' events if new opportunities seized	Not easy to plan for; possible budget issues

(d) How long will activities be?

Options	Advantages	Disadvantages
'One-off' activities Completed in one session	Often highly engaging with real 'wow' factor	Time-consuming to set up something new each session
	Could provide a product to take away	Limited continuity, so limited chances to improve work
	Useful at recruitment and launch events	Limited chance to work towards competitions or substantial projects
	If scattered throughout longer projects can be reinvigorating	If anyone misses a session, they miss the complete activity
	No loss of continuity if anyone misses sessions	
Short projects Activities that take 2–3 sessions to complete	Allows trying something before committing to longer projects	Limited depth to any one activity
	A chance to switch topics regularly	
Long projects Activities that take half a term or more to complete	Can be very rewarding, especially if awards or prizes involved	Not all students may sustain interest
	Deep involvement may generate lifelong interest	
Mixed-length activities and projects	Variety of approaches may appeal to many students	Students may have strong preferences for one activity and dislike imposed variation

(e) What age students should be involved?

Options	Advantages	Disadvantages
Same or similar ages	Activities can be chosen to match ages	No input from older students
	Suitable when working towards an age-related competition	Less exposure to a wider variety of perspectives
	May feel more secure for some students	May feel like lessons if with same groups of friends

(continued)

Table 4.2 (continued)

Options	Advantages	Disadvantages
Mixed ages	A wider pool of students to draw upon	Harder to find activities suiting interests and abilities of all students
	Siblings can work together	Older and younger students may not work well together
	Enhanced team-working opportunities; younger students could attempt projects too complex for their age but possible with older students' input	If one age group dominates, it may be off-putting for students of different ages
	Wider variety of perspectives, skills and knowledge	
	Older students, or those with more expertise, can act as mentors	
	Older students could help plan and deliver club activities; could add to their CV	
	Younger students could be extended by trying some of the older students' activities	
	Younger students might inspire older ones with fresh enthusiasm and enjoy doing jobs that older students find tedious	

(f) Who is the target audience?

Options	Advantages	Disadvantages
Interested and enthusiastic students	Enjoyable working with keen students	Enthusiasm may be unrealistic, e.g. blowing up the school or designing a robot to do homework. Creative STEM club leaders could channel such ambitions into realistic activities!
	Responsibility for ideas for sessions/projects could be given to the students. Ownership helps maintain motivation and could relieve staff of some planning pressures	Maintaining motivation could be problematic if initial expectations are not met
Gifted and talented (G&T)	Opportunities to challenge and extend students	May challenge staff to keep ahead of students, especially if novel projects involved or a student's interest is specific
	Potential to produce high-level outputs	May need additional mentors
	Could lead to publications and/or further research with collaborating industrial or academic contacts	May deter able students, unrecognised as G&T, yet with expertise in relevant areas
Mixed ability	Fairer and non-elitist	More challenging to provide activities motivating everyone and doable by all
	Wider variety of perspectives and skills	

| | Opportunities for mentoring and nurturing less able students | Some students may initially dominate, so important to assign roles and responsibilities early on |
| | Unrecognised gifts and talents, as well as enthusiasm, may be kindled in some students | |

(g) What rooms are wanted?

Options	Advantages	Disadvantages
Classroom	Less technical equipment around so may be safer environment than a lab	May recall atmosphere of lessons
	Familiarity with layout and means paper/pens can be found easily	Equipment available may be limited, though some could be imported if not too large/complex
	Food and drink may be allowable, creating more relaxed atmosphere	Tables may be fixed in place, restricting working arrangements
Laboratory	Already kitted out with safety features such as fume cupboards and resistant surfaces	Food and drink not allowed in labs, so another area needed if refreshments feature
	Most common equipment and materials likely to be on hand	Qualified staff may need to be present
	Logical venue for a Science club	Laboratory rules and regulations need to be known
		Appropriate risk assessments needed
		Staff from other departments may feel less confident working in labs
Computer suite	Logical venue for Computer Science or Programming clubs; also many STEM club activities	Food and drink not allowed in computer rooms, so another area needed if refreshments feature
	Students may appreciate using computers for their own ideas rather than carrying out set work	An IT technician may be needed to be 'on call'
	Students may be familiar with the facilities such as printers and scanners if a room they have used before	Passwords may be needed to be obtained
		Security features may restrict some uses
		Appropriate e-safety guidance necessary
Outdoor space	Essential for many environmental activities	Dependent on weather and seasons
	Most enjoy working outside, so could increase motivation	Appropriate risk assessments needed and safeguards put in place, including boundaries and potential hazards
	More space than available indoors for activities, such as rocket launching, that require plenty of room	May need a higher adult: student ratio than indoor activities
	More scope for 'extras' such as exploratory walks, bonfires, stargazing	Staff from other departments may feel less confident working outside

DBS, Disclosure and Barring Service.

Running a STEM club – successfully!

Naming your club

A good name for your STEM club will be needed at some point. You could wait until the first meeting and ask members to suggest suitable names or it might be useful to have a name already decided for use in marketing and advertising. The name could be functional/ descriptive or could be more imaginative and reflect something unique, to do with the school or locality.

Joining a STEM club network

Remember that others successfully run STEM clubs. It can be done! If your school has had a club that has stopped running, or is virtually inactive, try to find out the reasons. In this way, similar mistakes might be avoided.

By joining a network of STEM clubs you can see what others have done and get help and advice. In the UK the main organisation is the STEM clubs network. Networks tend to be national or regional bodies of mainly after-school clubs focusing on STEM subjects or topic-specific club networks, like Young Engineers Clubs, with their own programme of resources.

Membership of most of these networks is free, and benefits include online resources, advice, ideas and networking with teachers and other staff in similar positions. In the UK, practical support is also provided from dedicated regional STEM club advisors.

Once you have ideas about the type of club that you want to run, or even before, make good use of your regional STEM club advisor. These advisors have experiences of a variety of clubs and can tell you what is usually successful. They may also be able to give advice about 'off-the-shelf' packages of activities and other resources, including funding.

Creating a programme of activities

Drawing up a provisional programme of activities is helpful. This can be modified later, if the students want to take greater ownership of what they will be doing. Ownership increases motivation (Simmons and Page 2010) and increased motivation improves the chances of students continuing to attend.

Some ideas to consider in an initial programme might include:

- **Doing something dramatic** that has impact. An exciting practical or charismatic speaker is a possible attraction for a first session. Take photographs, with appropriate permissions. The activity could be advertised to ensure good attendance.
- **Writing up the first session.** By publicising the success of the first session, other students might not want to miss out next time. If students can write, or help write, an account for the school newsletter or website, so much the better. They can be given credit with their name on the article and perhaps encouraged to write more

in future. Add any suitable photographs for visual impact. Make sure the write-up gets to parents, so that the Parents' Association (or equivalent) may look kindly on requests for financial help in future. Make sure the account is printed and displayed in suitable venues for other students and staff to read and put on any monitor screens around school.

- **Including something for students to look forward to.** This could be a trip, certificate, award, competition entry or presentation. Having a concrete goal to aim towards might help retain members and avoid 'drop-out' after initial sessions.
- **Including something cross-curricular.** This makes it different from most lessons, may help to bring in more staff to help and might appeal to more students.
- **Making sure that more than one member of staff is involved.** That way, if one person is absent for any reason, the club session can continue.
- **Inviting in an expert,** possibly a STEM ambassador, either to help with and support the activities or to provide a stimulus or context with which to launch a project or series of activities.

Three examples of start-up programmes

There are lots of 'ready-to-go' programmes available online and via STEM club networks. Initial programmes could be modelled on one of these, as they are tried and tested. Examples are given in Boxes 4.1–4.3 of starter programmes for an Engineering club, an Animal club and a Maths and Art club.

Box 4.1   Be ENGineous activities (age 9–14 years)

Be ENGineous has been designed to give Young Engineers club leaders a ready-made programme to develop engineering skills of club members.

The programme provides a mix of activities relating to different branches of engineering. Each activity has three stages of difficulty, ranging from following instructions to research and development.

Activities include:

- Hovercrafts – General Engineering
- Bath bombs – Chemical Engineering
- FM radios – Electrical Engineering
- Water purification – Civil Engineering
- Putt putt boats – Marine Engineering
- Cranes – Mechanical Engineering
- Rambling robots – Robotic Engineering.

Box 4.2   Animal club (age 11–18 years) at lunchtime (40 minutes)

Session 1

Establish what live animals are available and hygiene rules; find out prior knowledge of attendees; split into groups, mixing older and younger students; and clean out enclosures of bearded dragon (*Pogona vitticeps*) and stick insects (*Carausius morosus*). Check outcomes, disposal of waste and handwashing.

Session 2

Feedback re session 1; find out career aspirations of attendees; observe bearded dragon in and out of enclosures for some initial behavioural studies; discuss future programme, including other animals students would like to work with; clean out enclosures and ask for suggestions about how the animals' environments could be enriched; include costs and reality checks. Handwashing.

Session 3

Clean out enclosures and implement some of the enrichment ideas for the habitats. Handwashing. Discuss how zoo animal habitats may be enriched via a 5-minute presentation from a 17-year-old student who had been a recipient of a Nuffield Science Bursary (now Nuffield Research Placements; see Box 5.2 in Chapter 5) and had monitored the seals and their enclosure at Bristol Zoo, UK, for her summer holiday project.

Further sessions arranged after discussion with students included: cleaning the teeth of a puppy owned by a staff member and a visit by a vet, a parent of one of the students, to talk about what got her interested in a veterinarian career.

Risk assessments were carried out for the animal handling.

Box 4.3   Maths and Art club (age 9–11 years) after school (45–60 minutes)

Maths and Art tend to be seen as separate subjects. The Maths and Art Network believes that 'often the beauty of maths can only be expressed through art'. Their programme for a Maths and Art club has 'an activity where you have to make something and most importantly to have fun' in each session. The first four sessions suggested are:

1   Mathematical magic show (including making a hole in a piece of paper big enough to walk through; *Möbius* strips and number tricks)
2   Mathematical origami
3   Making fractal pop-up cards
4   Flexagons.

Further ideas for start-up programmes could be to:

- use resources such as activities suggested for CREST Star or CREST Awards
- use a special day or event to launch the club. This could be the start of a National Science and Engineering Week or occasions such as Hallowe'en or an event linked to the school, such as a special anniversary or opening of a new/renovated building.

When drawing up your initial programme, try to include, for each session:

- staff names
- rooms
- times
- a list of the resources needed
- risk assessments/health and safety check
- cost implications.

Getting ready to launch your club

Once you have got a provisional programme together and an idea of your target membership, it may be wise at this stage to run your ideas past senior colleagues again (Figure 4.1) for final approval.

Share your programme with other staff, so that they are aware of what is intended and when.

- Pin up the programme in the staff room.
- Put the programme into a school newsletter.
- Email the programme to appropriate staff.
- Post the programme on the school website and on display screens if the school has these.

Making sure other staff are aware of a new activity helps avoid clashes with other events that might be in the process of being planned and might encourage offers of help from unexpected sources.

Now that you have got approval from senior management and other staff are aware of the existence of an exciting new venture, you need to make sure that you get a good turn-out of students for the first session. However, if this does not happen, news of successful events soon spreads and numbers are likely to build up for subsequent sessions. You may even find that you have to restrict numbers if events prove overly popular, so it is a good idea to know your maximum manageable number of students.

Chapter 5 gives more detailed ideas on advertising and marketing STEM clubs once they are up and running, but when advertising the existence of a new club, try to:

- invite students personally. This can be more effective than impersonal advertising and allows particular groups of students to be targeted
- display large, colourful posters advertising the 'what, when and where' of the new club. Choose places where students are likely to congregate and have time to read the poster. Figure 4.2 shows a poster used to advertise a STEM club

Figure 4.2 Poster advertising the STEM club at Baxter Business and Enterprise College, Kidderminster, UK, for the start of the 2012–2013 academic year.

Image courtesy of Science teacher, Mike Bullock. The club is for students aged 11–12 years. This image was previously published in Scott and Howarth (2012a).

- include advance notice in newsletters or via the school website. Open days for new students could target potential 'customers' and by alerting parents in plenty of time, they might encourage their offspring to attend, and have time to consider any alternative transport needs if students are going to finish later than usual
- get the new club mentioned in any assembly notices
- get staff to mention the new club in relevant lessons.

Finally, make yourself a checklist of what you are going to do. The checklist below might help.

Checklist for running a successful STEM club

The following checklist suggests key points to follow when running your club. Using this will not guarantee success, but should help.

Have clear aims and share these with members	
Keep a register and records of expenditure	
Have risk assessments for practical activities	
Involve as many staff as possible, particularly from more than one department	
Try to have helpers who are committed and enthusiastic; not easy when you have been teaching all day – hence a benefit of inviting experts in!	
Develop lists of fun practical activities and challenges	
Aim for an atmosphere different from lessons	
Agree a maximum number of students	
Be flexible and respond to members' needs, though be aware they may not know what these are until they try new things, so don't give in too easily	
Enter competitions and challenges even if the possibility of winning is remote. Taking part can be sufficient and certificates can always be created in house	
Take part in relevant events that involve days out, even if it means negotiating out-of-class time with other subject teachers; getting out and meeting other students, e.g. at STEM fairs, is invaluable	
Celebrate club successes and activities in school newsletters and local newspapers	
Try to get support from local STEM organisations	
Use invited experts/STEM ambassadors to support activities, launch new projects and talk about careers	
Bear in mind possible entrepreneurial outcomes	
Invite members of the Senior Management Team to attend sessions	
Register your STEM club with regional/national networks, e.g. STEMNET	
Make use of 'ready-made' resources, e.g. from professional bodies such as those provided by the Institute of Physics, at least at the start	
Ask members who attend regularly, and those who do not, for feedback to find out what they really enjoy to help future planning	

Extending and enhancing STEM clubs

Making clubs sustainable

By the end of this chapter, you will have information and ideas about how to:

- extend an existing STEM club
- enhance your STEM club
- make your STEM club sustainable.

Your STEM club is up and running, that is good news. However, students' initial enthusiasm can take a dip when the novelty of a new club wears off. Strategies may be needed to keep the club going and to continue to make it attractive for students, so that every student wants to attend, parents like talking about what their children get out of attending, local employers discuss it and the Head wants to give you promotion. This chapter cannot promise or provide all of the above, but the intent is to give practical ideas, examples and some case studies to help you on the way.

EXTENDING EXISTING STEM CLUBS

One way of ensuring that a club remains viable may be to make it bigger. Expanding too much too quickly has dangers if resources, people included, are spread too thinly. However, larger clubs can be more sustainable as they are able to absorb changes in students attending or staff helping to run them.

Enthusiastic STEM club leaders are just the sort of people who get promotion, so having several staff involved in running the club helps cover staffing changes. Note that it is perfectly possible to run small clubs – some with three to four students operate successfully, but perhaps in a limited manner.

To extend a club you could:

1 increase recruitment generally by
   a   widening the age range
   b   increasing recruitment from minority groups
2 increase the number and variety of people running the club
3 change the number and/or length of sessions
4 increase the range of activities.

Widening the age range of members

Many STEM clubs mainly attract younger students, perhaps ages 11–14 years, in secondary schools. Students aged 16+, if they join anything, tend to join specialist clubs that suit their studies and career options, or get involved as helpers.

In primary schools, the focus for STEM clubs seems to be towards the top end, with mainly students aged 10–11 participating; younger students appear not to be represented significantly.

Of course, the above statements are generalisations and there are schools where the picture is quite different, but we have observed this to be the current case for many schools in England.

There are advantages in working with similar-aged students, but there are possibly more advantages in having a wide age range of members. This is shown in Table 4.2 in Chapter 4.

Some strategies for widening the age range of students attending a STEM club are suggested in Table 5.1. This table refers to Case Studies 5.1–5.3.

Some suggestions involve outside help. Chapter 7 has information about making sure that it is safe to invite visitors.

Table 5.1 Strategies for widening the age range of students in a STEM club

Aim: To include more students . . .	Suggested strategies Note: some extend beyond the given phase
Across a wide age range, e.g. 5–11 years	Bring in more help. The adult/child ratio requirement for younger students is usually higher than for older students. Additional helpers could be: • STEM ambassadors • Parents • Older siblings • Older students who have moved up a school and/or who may be interested as part of the 'service' element of the Duke of Edinburgh Award scheme • Work experience students. Students considering a career in teaching may like to work with 5–11-year-olds. Contact local secondary schools to raise awareness of this opportunity • Undergraduates. Some universities offer education modules as part of degree courses and some undergraduates may be keen to gain experience of working with the younger age range Involve additional helpers in planning, so that they feel involved Use projects involving a range of skills so all can be involved in appropriately challenging activities Work towards accredited awards such as those offered by CREST Star
Across a wide age range, e.g. 11–18 years	Use STEM ambassadors or other expert help (see above) Make roles and responsibilities clear, with well-defined ground rules Involve students in planning so they have 'ownership' of projects Develop opportunities for older students to mentor younger ones Use activities, with differentiated outcomes, to appeal to all age ranges; these could be linked by a theme Relate activities to the 'real world' so students see the relevance Consider using CREST Awards (see Box 2.2 in Chapter 2) See Case Study 5.1

(continued)

Table 5.1 (continued)

Aim: To include more students...	Suggested strategies Note: some extend beyond the given phase
Across two school phases	Choose a project that students can see has mutual benefits, such as designing improvements for a shared open space, perhaps a garden. This would involve all the STEM areas (Scott and Howarth 2012b)
	Encourage older, ex-students to return and help; they could help plan or be given a responsible role such as a group 'leader'
	Invite prospective students to visit their future school, not just for a one-off open event, but on a regular basis or for a summer school
	See Case Studies 5.2 and 5.3
Aged 14–16 years	Build on any bronze CREST Awards with potential for silver
	Make projects 'cool' to suit teenagers. A cosmetics club may appeal to some (investigate The Royal Institution of Great Britain, L'Oreal Cosmetics Centre)
	Use partnership grants schemes (e.g. offered by the Royal Society) to run projects with professional scientists or engineers
	Provide snacks, if funding available; rapidly growing teenagers are always hungry; assisting teachers may also appreciate these
	Consider activities linked to television programmes e.g. forensic science links to the long-running 'CSI'
	Invite well-known people. With notice, personalities connected with STEM may visit and enthuse students for free, especially if they have any connections with the locality. Find out if • the school/region has any famous alumni with STEM connections • your nearest universities employ academics with STEM Communication roles such as Alice Roberts, Professor of Public Engagement in Science, at the University of Birmingham
Aged 16–18 years	Older students are likely to be focused on 1. school leaving exams 2. the next stage of their education 3. their future career
	Offer activities that help with these aspirations: 1. For students focused on passing exams Make activities exam-related: • do practical work to illustrate theories • do further practical work to allow practising particular skills • have talks or workshops to clarify, illustrate or extend aspects of STEM on which they will be examined
	With all of these activities, try and retain a club atmosphere so that they don't feel like revision workshops

2. For students focused on the next stage of their education

Provide activities to enhance CVs and improve chances of acceptance into further/higher education. Encourage students to:

- work towards gold CREST Awards (Chapter 2, Box 2.2)
- apply for Nuffield Research Placements (Box 5.2, this chapter)
- work on projects that could be 'show-cased' at Young Engineer/ Young Scientist Fairs
- take responsibility, leading in project areas or helping run a club for younger students, perhaps part of a Duke of Edinburgh Award

Provide information relevant to education beyond school by inviting speakers/presenters to extend students' current knowledge (Chapter 2, Box 2.1 has information about finding speakers)

3. For students focused on future careers

Make activities ones that relate to the world of work:

- Invite speakers to talk about particular STEM careers
- Provide experiences of skills likely to be relevant. For example, projects linked to entrepreneurship or involving communication
- Visit industries or companies

For all activities, avoid clashing with revision periods and exam weeks

---

CASE STUDY 5.1   Involving a wide age range of students

The Fossil Club, Thomas Hardye School, Dorchester

The Fossil Club, at the Thomas Hardye School, Dorchester, UK, successfully involves a wide age range of students, from 13 to 19 years old. The club uses a variety of cross-curricular activities and involves many members of the school, including parents. In 2011, the club put on a stunning display at The Big Bang: UK Young Scientists' and Engineers' Fair in London (Howarth and Scott 2011a).

The club started with a rock with an odd bit protruding. Using Chemistry to extract the 'bit', later identified as a fossil, the club quickly became interdisciplinary, with activities linking fossils to music, photography, drama, poetry and family fun days. Middle school pupils (9–13 years) were involved. Tracy Chevalier visited and discussed her book, *Remarkable Creatures*, about Mary Anning, the early fossil collector (Chevalier 2010).

Club members work on activities at lunchtimes and after school. The club has started to share best practice by making films and creating a booklet of poems about fossils (Thomas Hardye School 2010). The school has a very successful track record in the National Science and Engineering Competition, with one student becoming Young Scientist of the Year in 2010. In 2012–2013, the school's website showed 13 different STEM clubs.

CASE STUDY 5.2   Summer STEM school for prospective students

The Warwick School, Surrey

An 8-day summer holiday programme aimed to ease transition from primary to secondary school for 10–11-year-olds.

The programme consists of enjoyable, but purposeful, activities, such as:

- Rockets – simulations and competitions
- Space – 'do aliens exist' discussion, investigating 'ice cores from planets', building and programming a Mars Rover using Lego Mindstorm kits and observatory visit
- Time – making sun dials and investigating pendulums as measuring devices
- Biodiversity – activities run by Wildlife Trust: pond-dipping, making nettle string and charcoal pencils
- Senses – making perfumes; 'Dragon's Den' to 'pitch' their product; careers talk
- Where in the World – endangered species, sources of precious metals
- Forensics and Shakespeare – who killed Macbeth? Deductive reasoning and investigating
- Presentation to parents – short drama with scenery, backdrop and music. A special edition of the school's newsletter and certificates given out.

The summer school brings additional benefits: extra resources, a growing network of contacts, ideas for activities, staff development and stronger working relationships between staff from different departments as well as good publicity.

Further details in Carter (2013).

CASE STUDY 5.3   An example of a cross-phase STEM activity

Young Engineers 'Making Knexions' Project

This initiative helps secondary schools link with 'feeder' primary schools via STEM activities. Primary students gain mentors and older students gain mentoring experience.

The project takes 2.5+ hours and generally involves a team of six to ten primary students, aged 9–11, ideally with one older student mentor. The K'Nex materials (plastic construction parts) may be borrowed for free by state-supported schools. Postage is also free if two school phases are involved. An explanatory pack for teachers is available.

The overall theme of the 'Making Knexions' project is Sustainable Engineering. Three modules are set in different environments: agriculture, inner city and maritime.

Students research, design, plan, cost and develop a solution to a problem and then build their final design out of K'Nex parts. Each module encourages students to learn about structures and renewable energy, as well as work with younger/older students.

Increasing recruitment from minority groups

There is evidence that some groups are poorly represented in STEM careers (Tyson *et al.* 2007; Future Morph 2011; National Action Council for Minorities in Engineering 2012). These groups include:

- black and minority ethnic
- those from a family with no history of higher education
- girls
- white boys from underprivileged backgrounds
- those who are disabled.

The Equality Act (2010) promotes equality across a range of protected characteristics. Schools are expected to comply with the requirements and make every effort to ensure that minority groups participate in all areas. The 'all areas' includes STEM clubs, so you need to consider whether membership of your club is inclusive.

The maximum amount of Science that students in England, aged 14–16, study for examination is 'Triple Science' or equivalent. Triple Science is less available in schools in areas of higher deprivation (House of Commons Report 2011b), so students from these schools may have limited access to study Science.

Encouraging students from minority groups to participate in STEM clubs provides opportunities to redress reduced levels of academic study and other missed experiences. It could alter perceptions of available careers and eventual career choices. Chapter 6 discusses supporting equal opportunities through STEM careers advice. The online STEM Equality and Diversity Toolkit is also highly recommended (see Chapter 9).

Some suggestions for recruiting and retaining students from minority groups include:

- Hold special events for particular groups, e.g. girls only. Consider a girls-only club. This is successful elsewhere, e.g. Girls Excelling in Maths and Science (GEMS) club.
- Use role models. Black and minority ethnic students are significantly disadvantaged by a lack of relevant role models (Rasekoala 2001). However, take care not to overglamorise roles. Ultrafeminine Maths and Science role models apparently demotivate girls; being feminine and successful in a STEM role appears impossible to some girls (Wadley 2012). Portraying female STEM roles as everyday ones may be more effective and could be achieved by giving girls opportunities to meet female STEM ambassadors and learn about their career paths.

    There is also evidence (Hoxbury and Avery 2012) that, without role models, high-achieving, low-income students are more likely to apply to less selective colleges.
- Ensure that images of people used in posters/presentations have a good mix of minority groups.
- Make use of any minority group staff or senior students interested in helping out with the club.
- Send club programmes to parents of students who might particularly benefit from being involved in the club, with translations if appropriate.
- Include activities that students see as relevant. Springate *et al.* (2008) suggest key factors in encouraging ethnic minority students to continue with STEM were passion for the subjects and positive perceptions about the relevance of subjects and careers.

Number and variety of people running the club: STEM leadership qualification

Team efforts in running STEM clubs are generally more sustainable than solo efforts. Use the checklist in Table 5.2 to consider who might be invited to help plan and/or run your club.

It may not be obvious to include non-STEM teaching staff on this list, but the Head of French may be a keen astronomer and a Music teacher may have done a joint Music and Maths degree. Historians are often interested in the History of Medicine. Geographers have valuable knowledge of Geology and Environmental issues. Staff without STEM backgrounds may be interested to learn along with students, so it is worth letting all staff know help is wanted.

Some staff may be reluctant to take part due to anxieties about subject knowledge or competence with particular activities. Various training schemes are available, many free, for people helping run STEM clubs. Chapter 3 and the final section of this chapter have further information.

Involving students in planning and running the club allows them to experience responsibility, teaching and mentoring. They could research speakers, write invitations and 'thank yous' and look after visitors. This will enhance their CV and further education/job

Table 5.2 Checklist of people to help run a club

Who could help?	Already involved	Could be invited
STEM teaching staff, including trainee teachers		
STEM teaching or learning support assistants		
Science and Technology lab technicians		
Non-STEM teaching staff		
Other staff, e.g. gardeners, cooks		
Governors		
Older students, from the same school, from the next school phase up or from college/university		
Students doing a STEM leadership qualification		
Parents/guardians		
Grandparents/other relatives		
STEM ambassadors		
STEM club advisor from STEM club network		
Local STEM professionals working in industries or academia		
Retired people who have had STEM careers		

opportunities and raise their self-esteem. If in doubt about trusting students, there is a wonderful paragraph, in a blog about teaching disengaged boys, by a Head from York: 'Choose your moment and use the phrase, *I'm going to trust you to do this*, looking directly into their eyes. It works' (Tomsett 2012).

Students, aged 14–16, can work towards a BTEC (work-related, currently non-examined) STEM leadership qualification. This aims to:

> develop, test and challenge learners' leadership capabilities through practical, engaging and inspiring self-driven opportunities. The balanced learning programme concentrates on developing their collaborative and thinking skills in STEM as well as enhancing self-awareness and a belief in their own abilities.
>
> (Pearson Education 2012)

Students studying for this qualification would make useful additions to STEM club teams.

Changing the number and/or length of sessions

One way of extending STEM clubs is to have more sessions. This may be necessary if large numbers of students want to attend. Rather than a problem, this should be viewed as success!

Putting on more sessions needs careful consideration. Table 4.2 in Chapter 4 suggests advantages and disadvantages of different frequencies of club sessions when deciding on setting up a STEM club.

Table 5.3 suggests some issues and solutions when considering more sessions.

Table 4.2 in Chapter 4 describes advantages and disadvantages of different session lengths when setting up STEM clubs. As student and staff commitment and interest grow,

Table 5.3 More sessions: issues and solutions

Issue	Pros	Cons – and solutions
Staff time	If staff take turns in running sessions, more gain experience	More staff needed or a heavier 'workload' for the same people
		Training may help
Rooms	Greater room use could lead to more 'presence', e.g. wall displays	Enough suitable rooms needed
		Advance booking should help
Costs	Bulk-buying can be more cost-effective	Doubling up sessions could double costs of materials and (if provided) refreshments
		Students purchase or bring their own refreshments
Attendance	Repeated sessions might improve attendance if choice given	Uneven attendance makes equipment and materials difficult to cater for; advance registers could help
Club profile	More sessions will raise club's profile; more to report and more students involved	None, unless resources stretched and feedback starts to be poor. Avoid this by listening to students and acting on feedback

longer sessions may become appropriate and give time for more meaningful projects. Many of the points in Table 5.3 apply when considering the pros and cons of longer sessions. Additionally, do consider letting the caretaker/janitor know so that you don't get locked in after everyone else has gone home!

In rural schools, it can be difficult to hold after-school clubs due to use of school buses. In these circumstances, it may be better to focus on shorter lunchtime sessions.

Increasing the number and range of activities

Increasing the number and range of activities may widen the appeal of clubs and so increase recruitment. It could have the opposite effect for some students with specific passions, e.g. for chess, so before making changes do ask the students.

Some schools run STEM clubs rotating between Science, Design & Technology and Maths/ICT. This spreads workload and gives teachers preparation time and opportunities to learn from each other's sessions.

A club with unusually diverse activities is showcased in Case Study 5.1 on page 73.

One way of increasing the range of activities could be to ensure the Maths component is incorporated whenever appropriate. The following section has some suggestions on how to do this.

Putting the M into STEM

A cause for concern, in some STEM clubs, is how to engage with Maths (STEMNET 2013). Another concern is that STEM can become STE + M (Museum of Science, Boston 2013).

Potential solutions include:

- involve a mathematician in planning the activities
- invite mathematicians to help run activities
- look for the Maths present in most projects. Members of an Animal club used maths in:
  - o   recording expenditure on animal food
  - o   weighing animals and drawing graphs of their gain in mass
  - o   calculating speed of African land snails, *Achatina fulica*.

Another way of increasing the range of activities could be linking with other schools.

Linking with other schools

Working with other schools might mean that more specialised facilities or equipment are available. Greater numbers of potential members could make buying materials more cost-effective. The cost of coaches for trips could also be shared. Students and staff from different schools are likely to have different areas of expertise and so could bring a wider variety of perspectives to planning sessions.

Linking with a STEM club of an overseas school could be exciting and enriching, with benefits to both clubs. Box 5.1 outlines two schemes that help link schools.

Box 5.1   Examples of schemes that help link schools

Connecting classrooms

The British Council and the British Science Association are working together to enrich STEM activities in the UK and abroad, through a programme called Connecting Classrooms.

Benefits include:

- sharing learning and teaching with other teachers internationally
- putting STEM into global contexts
- a £1,500 grant to visit your overseas partner school.

At the time of writing, 30+ schools in Bangladesh were looking for UK partners to share STEM learning.

Further information is available from the British Science Association website, Connecting Classrooms pages.

Science Across the World

This programme, organised by the Association for Science Education in partnership with BP and GSK, has won international awards. Schools communicate with each other via social networking sites and virtual learning environments. Steps are provided to help set up links and specific topics advocated, mainly ones that deal with aspects of Science that produce differences across the world. Examples include:

- Eating and Drinking; Plants and Me (8–12-year-olds)
- Biodiversity Around Us; Drinking Water (12–17-year-olds).

All the topics could make great STEM club activities and are freely available from the eLibrary of the National STEM Centre. Most topics are available in other languages.

ENHANCING STEM CLUBS

The previous section considered extending clubs by increasing sessions, participants, leaders and activities. It is also useful to consider the quality of what is on offer. This section looks at ways of enhancing STEM clubs by considering successful programmes, outcomes and publicity.

Successful programmes

A programme could be judged to be successful if club members keep returning and membership grows. Another measure of success is increased uptake of STEM subjects within school and more applications to study STEM in further or higher education. Equally important are any increases in positive attitudes towards STEM.

Some ideas to make programmes successful include the following.

Advance planning

- Plan ahead so sessions are more likely to run smoothly.
- Order equipment and materials well in advance.
- Advertise the programme so helpers and participants know dates/times and are less likely to book alternative activities.

Tried and tested projects

- Use projects that have been done before and shown to work. Things working well motivate students.
- Choose projects with elements of risk to appeal to students, such as the challenge to deliver unbroken eggs using parachutes or catapults. This is 'eggciting', especially if uncooked eggs are used, and creative.
- Use available advice on running projects successfully, e.g. the BBC's Great Egg Race archive.
- Check Chapter 11 for examples of projects.

Novel projects

The section above recommends trying 'safe' activities so that there is a degree of certainty that they will work. Students also enjoy novel projects. Anything not delivered via the curriculum is likely to be perceived as novel.

Try mixing subjects with projects linking:

- **Science** and **Art**: creating tattoos, via oxidation, on bananas (Instructables 2013)
- Performing Arts and STEM subjects: e.g. the Institute of Physics Ashfield Music Festival – developing enterprise skills and learning applications of Physics in setting up music festivals (IoP website, Ashfield pages)
- **Food** Technology and **Engineering**: building chocolate bridges, demonstrated by the Welding Institute at The Big Bang Fair (Howarth and Scott 2012)
- **Languages** and **Textiles**: working together to plan a trip, such as to the Textile Museum, Musée de la Mode et du Textile, in Paris.

Introduce subjects and topics from beyond the curriculum. For example:

- **Archaeology** is currently popular, perhaps due to television programmes such as Time Team (Newnham 2008). The National STEM Centre collection includes Young Archaeologists Club activities. Two examples that could be used successfully in STEM clubs are:
  o   Design and build a roundhouse.
  o   Fake poo. Students investigate diets of ancient cultures using safe 'fake poo'. Recipes are given for making Aztec, Viking, Roman and Tudor 'poo'. By examining the 'poo' contents, students identify differences in the diets of these cultures.
- **Forensic Science** is also popular and could involve investigations, perhaps using ideas from the CSI television series but substituting local place names and real names of

people. Suitable for all ages and abilities. High View Primary Learning Centre in Yorkshire has run a Forensic Science Club for 9–11-year-olds where students learned about fingerprinting, serology, hair and bone analysis and fibre identification.

- **Polar Studies**: the 'Cool Club' for younger students is described in 'Polar science is cool' (Weeks 2012). For older students there are various opportunities; for example, EducaPoles, the educational website of The International Polar Foundation, has activities about polar regions linked to energy and biodiversity.

'Big impact' sessions

One-off activities, completed in single sessions, can have a real impact. Though possibly more time-consuming to organise than projects lasting several sessions, their highly engaging nature is of great value in injecting renewed enthusiasm into a programme. Suggestions include:

- Invite commercial STEM performers to give a 'magic science show' or similar. These are likely to cost a lot so be prepared to sell tickets to non-club members or seek funding.
- Invite non-commercial STEM ambassadors in to give a workshop about something special.
- Put on special workshops to make specific products that can be taken away at the end. This could be a necklace containing students' own DNA (Bio-Rad offers a kit for 36 students for £113; the activity takes 90 minutes) or cup cakes with personalised, computer-printed icing layers using edible printer inks (Donna 2012).

Special days/weeks/events/celebrations

Two articles in *School Science Review* list potential events that could be used to create special STEM club sessions (Howarth and Scott 2011b; Scott and Howarth 2011). Although some of the dates are specific to a particular year, dates for future years could easily be found.

Real research

It is possible to carry out research, via extra STEM opportunities, producing new information, sometimes worth publishing. This is true for all ages of students.

1   Primary school example. In 2010, *Biology Letters*, the journal of the Royal Society, published a paper online by a class of 8–10-year-olds from a school in Devon (Blackawton 2010), followed by a print version (Blackawton 2011). This was the first peer-reviewed scientific paper published in a top journal by such young authors. Their project, about vision in bumblebees, mentored by Beau Lotto (Lotto 2011), attracted attention worldwide. The project was so inspiring that it led to the creation of the 'i,scientist' programme based in the Science Museum, London (Arnold 2010; Lotto 2011). Two years later, one of the pupils from the original project, then aged 12, discussed the research on a TED talk (Lotto and O'Toole 2012).

2   Secondary school example. A Nuffield Science bursary (now Nuffield Research Placement) allowed Jessica Birt, then about to start her final year in a school in Chester, to undertake a project on the behaviour of giant otters (*Ptenonura brasiliensis*). Jessica's research, at Chester Zoological Gardens, resulted in the zoo planning to create a new

underwater tunnel to view the otters and, for herself, the runner-up prize for the Young Scientist of the Year. Jessica said:

> No matter what course [at university] you want to do, especially if you have interviews, doing a project like this can give you something to talk about . . . I can't believe that the zoo is building a tunnel because of the research I did – they still ring me up as I know more about these particular rare otters than anyone else.

(Howarth and Scott 2011a)

Box 5.2 describes two schemes providing placement opportunities for older students.

Box 5.2   Examples of schemes providing placement opportunities for older students

Nuffield Research Placements (previously Nuffield Science bursaries)

These placements provide over 1,000 UK students each year with opportunities to work alongside STEM professionals. All students studying a STEM subject, in the first year of post-16 courses, are eligible. Placements may be in universities, research institutions, commercial companies or voluntary organisations and occur during the summer holidays. Students must give up 4–6 weeks of their holiday, but rewards can include opportunities to:

- gain insights into current research and development
- get first-hand experience of STEM in working environments
- see 'real world' applications of their school studies
- gain gold CREST Awards
- enhance their CV
- make useful contacts
- attend regional celebration events.

For some, the rewards may extend to:

- having their names on publications
- winning further awards, potentially Young Scientist or Young Engineer of the Year.

Students without a family history of attending university or who attend schools in less well-off areas are particularly encouraged to apply for placements. No one is excluded on a financial basis. Students' travel costs are covered and some students may be eligible for weekly bursaries.

   Examples of previous project titles can be found in Chapter 11. The Nuffield Research Placement website has further information.

In2scienceUK

This organisation provides placements for gifted A-level students from low-income backgrounds. The scheme aims to use 'the commitment, passion and experience of scientists to ensure the brightest pupils have the opportunity to experience research science first hand, regardless of their wealth'.

Placements take place over the summer. Working alongside practising scientists gives students an insight into scientific research.

For more information, see the In2scienceUK website.

Respond to changing interests

Acting on informal feedback or formal evaluations should help to maintain a programme that appeals to participants.

As students mature, the focus and challenge of activities may need to change. Involving students in planning the programme should help to create popular events and a sense of ownership amongst the students that increases recruitment and retention.

Consider starting a new club with a different focus. If a STEM club for 11–12-year-olds has lots of 'wow' activities, then it might be appropriate to have a club for 13–14-year-olds with potential for longer project work.

Take advantage of contemporary events. Every year there will be meteorite showers, new applications of smart materials, new environmental challenges – lots of things for clubs to explore.

Remember that you are more likely to be aware of new initiatives than most students, so watch out for new opportunities.

Have fun!

Few will attend optional clubs unless they enjoy what goes on. This includes staff. Some key points include:

- food
- music
- location
- trips
- inspiring activities.

A basic rule, especially for after-school clubs, must be to 'feed and water' attendees. Staff, students and visitors respond well to being looked after, even if it is only a chance to eat or drink what they have brought along themselves. Time and a suitable place for refreshments need to be allowed for as lab, technology or computer-based activities don't mix well with eating.

Consider using music as background for activities that won't be disrupted by additional noise. It may be necessary to try and find a genre that pleases everyone – the 'wrong' kind of music may be worse than no music at all.

Use different locations if activities allow this. Chapter 3 has suggestions of school areas that could be used for STEM activities. For younger students, using rooms or facilities normally reserved for older students can be exciting. For older students, a visit back to their previous school could be enjoyable. Outdoor locations featured highly in the entries for the 2012–2013 competition where school students designed 'The School We'd Like' (Guardian 2013).

Consider trips away from school. Chapter 3 discusses the pros and cons of going on visits to extend the curriculum; visits can also be relevant in enhancing a STEM Club Programme.

Make activities enjoyable. There are ideas earlier in this chapter and elsewhere throughout the book for inspiring activities. Chapter 9 lists resources and books providing ideas for activities. Chapter 11 has lists of engaging activities. Specialist organisations can suggest good ideas. The British Science Association has over 300 activities for under- and over-11-year-olds, including a Science Busking Pack, suitable for all ages (see Chapter 9). The STEM clubs network has many examples of activities (Stem Clubs 2013).

Successful outcomes

Having specific outcomes increases motivation and retention of club members as they see particular targets ahead and that each session has a purpose, leading towards this final outcome. It is perfectly possible to run a STEM club without specific outcomes, for example a series of 'one-off' events, but having a target can be helpful. The executive summary of the Afterschool Alliance (2013) report, *Defining Youth Outcomes for STEM Learning in Afterschool*, recommended that 'it is important to set appropriate and flexible goals'.

Actual outcomes may vary depending on the nature of the group but could be one or more of the following.

Awards

- CREST Star Investigator Award
- CREST Award: bronze, silver or gold
- STEM club leadership qualification
- Certificate for completing a challenge, taking part in an event or competition
- Prize for winning a competition.

Presentations

- To junior schools, parents, school assembly, perhaps during National Science and Engineering Week
- To internal judges for bronze CREST Awards
- To external judges as part of silver or gold CREST Awards
- To external judges at regional or national finals, such as The Big Bang Fair or the National Science and Engineering Competition
- To showcase the STEM club at The Big Bang or The Big Bang Near Me (regional fairs).

Products

- Items to sell at parents' evenings
- Working models such as the unique student 'hamster wheel' demonstrated at The Big Bang in 2011 (Figure 5.1)
- Electronic products such as the portable drum kit trousers displayed and played by Aseem Mishra, Young Engineer for Britain, 2010

Figure 5.1   The student hamster wheel was popular at The Big Bang: UK Young Scientists' and Engineers' Fair, 2011. Designed, made and trialled by students ages 14–15 years from the Carbon Neutral Club, Hitchin Girls School, Hertfordshire, the wheel uses human power to generate up to 200 watts of electricity, enough to provide lights for a household if the human hamster can keep going. When asked what the school intends to do with the wheel, the response was: 'Keep it for charity days and detentions!'

This picture was previously published in *School Science Review* (Howarth and Scott 2011a).

- Scrapbooks or portfolios of investigations
- Films, booklets, blogs, podcasts
- Articles for school newsletters or websites
- A scientific paper (Lotto 2011).

Whatever the outcomes, try to showcase your club's efforts in some way. This could be just for the school and those connected with the school, such as parents and governors. Or it could be an external event, such as a STEM fair. Chapter 3 discusses STEM fairs and festivals.

Benefits to students include:

- increased confidence and self-esteem
- evidence that their work is worth showing to others
- a chance to represent their club or school
- an increased chance of networking with others interested in similar areas – this could be other schools, parents, possible employers, contacts from industry/academia
- a chance for students to add to their CV and/or college or university application.

Successful publicity

Having a great programme and inspirational outcomes will undoubtedly help in creating a successful STEM club, but unless you make good use of suitable publicity, no one will know! And if no one knows about the good things happening, it may be harder to get support from the School Leadership Team, harder to get funding and harder to recruit new members.

Chapter 3 discusses advertising new STEM clubs. This section has further ideas about publicity, including marketing strategies for STEM clubs that are up and running. Some of the suggested strategies could be delegated to student members to involve them in promoting their own club and give them the opportunity to be creative and add their own ideas.

Strategies to publicise and market your STEM club

- **Get the club's programme into the school's calendar** of events. This will remind students, staff and parents and may help to avoid clashes with other events.
- **Make lists of all the good things** that have happened during club sessions and beyond, including attending STEM fairs. Send copies to the Senior Leadership Team, Head, members and staff helpers. Pin a copy to a staffroom noticeboard. Ask for the list to be included in the next school newsletter and be posted on the school's website.
- **Know your audience.** Be aware of who is interested in the club's activities. Use Table 5.1 as a checklist.
- **Print leaflets.** Involve the students in designing these. Leaflets are useful for open days, parents' events or times when school clubs are promoted to new or returning students.
- **Create lively posters** advertising the club. Involve students in designing these.
- **Ask for a noticeboard** to showcase the club's events and successes. Locate it where students and visitors are likely to read it. Make it visually attractive and keep it up to date. Perhaps students could be in charge of the noticeboard.
- **Ask for a page on the school's website** to showcase the club. This could be useful to list last-minute changes or opportunities and to let parents know what is happening, when. Post photos (with permission) of activities. Include items written by club members and quotes.
- **Take photos or videos.** Make sure that suitable permission is given before taking and using photographs or videos of students and staff. Use these on web pages about the club's activities.
- **Get quotes.** These could be from student members, helpers, visitors or others. Ask permission to use them. Ask students to complete an evaluation. This is likely to generate usable quotes. Quotes enliven web pages and could be useful in obtaining funding.
- **Ask for a paragraph on the school newsletter to be reserved** for an update on the club's activities; that way, you get regular reminders about deadline intervals to prompt you into writing.
- **Make the programme public.** Put it on the school website and elsewhere. Make the programme look attractive in content and in layout.
- **Talk about the club** – to your students in lessons, to other staff in the school, to parents at parents' evening, to other teachers from other schools, via online discussion groups.
- **Write about the club.** This could be a project to add to the STEM club network database or a student's article for the school magazine (Figure 5.2). An article could also be written for a professional association's web pages or journal. *School Science Review* is interested in short or long articles about STEM club activities and has a dedicated section called 'The Clubbers' Guide'.

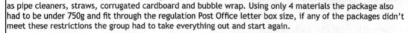

NATIONAL SCIENCE AND ENGINEERING WEEK

The Post a Pringle Project **Year 7**

This year and every year for the last decade there has been a opportunity for secondary school children to take part in National Science and Engineering week and so have fun in science lessons. This year Year 7 did the 'Post a Pringle Project'.

The idea of the project was to design a package that would stop a Pringle from getting broken if it was posted to our homes.

All lessons started with a brief demonstration on what to do and how to do it. We had access to a range of materials such as pipe cleaners, straws, corrugated cardboard and bubble wrap. Using only 4 materials the package also had to be under 750g and fit through the regulation Post Office letter box size, if any of the packages didn't meet these restrictions the group had to take everything out and start again.

All the forms were split up into 5 groups all to make one package that would later be posted to one group member's house, who would then bring it to school for the following lesson where they would reveal if their pringle had broken or not. Once the teams started to make the packaging it became clear that the challenge would not be as straightforward as they had first anticipated. In our form taught by Miss Oliver only 1 pringle survived.

A week later, with all the Pringles returned, the winners of the year 7 'Post a Pringle Project' were revealed, a draw between 7M and 7S with 1 pringle each returned. Now everyone's attention is turning to next years National Science and Engineering week and more importantly the winner of the Year 7 science week competition!

Courteney Boden 7H

Figure 5.2 An article written by a student, aged 12, that appeared in her school newsletter, May 2012. The article is about an activity she had taken part in for the National Science and Engineering Week. Thanks to Hayley Oliver, student teacher, who encouraged Courteney to write this and who supplied a copy of the article. (Pringles is a brand of potato- and wheat-based snacks, owned by the Kellogg Company. The individual pieces are curved with ridges and sold stacked in tubes. Their uniform shape and size make them ideal for testing. The 'Post a Pringle' activity is based on the Science Museum's 'SOS – Save Our Snacks' activity.)

The photo and text have been previously published in *School Science Review* (Scott and Howarth 2012a).

- **Hold occasional special events.** Invite non-members, staff and parents. Have a special speaker or a presenter running a workshop. Give plenty of advance publicity and ensure the event is written up afterwards. Ask someone to take photographs.
- **Let local newspapers and radio know** about any special events or awards/competitions won by members; they are often looking for news items and likely to be delighted to be contacted. Follow school guidance about contacting the media; there may be a nominated person who acts as external media officer.
- **Celebrate prizes, awards or finishing projects.** Use any or all of the above strategies to publicise student achievements, but also have a celebration during a club session.

MAKING A STEM CLUB SUSTAINABLE

A sustainable club could be defined as one that continues without draining the school's resources or the energy of the people responsible for running it. For clubs running over long periods, such as a school term or a year, issues of whether the club can be sustained need addressing early on.

The London Engineering Programme website has information about club sustainability (see Chapter 9) and this has contributed to the ideas in the following section.

Key issues

Staffing

Enough staff

The more staff involved in the STEM club, the stronger the club will be. There should be enough staff to cover absences or someone leaving. If many sessions are cancelled, then the sustainability of the club could be in question.

Realistic appraisal of staff members' other commitments could be undertaken before giving them roles in running a club. No one likes starting something and then giving up, but this could happen with enthusiastic volunteers, such as newly qualified teachers, who may not appreciate the implications of taking on additional duties.

In an ideal world, some time allowance, in the form of a reduced teaching timetable, ought to be given to those who help with clubs, taking into account preparation and contact time. This is currently not usual and most staff support students out of personal enthusiasm and generosity.

Enough expert staff

Lovely though it is to have many helping hands, for some clubs this is not enough. Some activities, such as the CREST Star Investigators activities, come with full instructions and state that no expertise is needed, but most clubs will benefit from having knowledgeable experts. Some clubs may not be able to run without these or the range of activities offered may be severely limited.

If experts are not available, then training may be the solution. Some examples of organisations offering free training for STEM club leaders or for teaching STEM outside the classroom are:

- The STEM club network offers STEM club leader training in the form of STEM 'TeachMeets' – so far, only in some regions.
- The Institute of Electrical and Electronics Engineers Teacher In-Service Program enables volunteers to share technical expertise and demonstrate applications of engineering concepts to support teaching and learning of Science, Mathematics and Technology (see Chapter 9).
- The Royal Academy of Engineering has professional development sessions for STEM club leaders for both Design & Technology and Engineering.
- Some professional associations, such as the Institute of Physics, run workshops, often locally and often free.

Chapter 3 has information about STEM professional development opportunities. In England and Wales, your local STEM club advisor may also be able to help with training or finding training opportunities.

Membership

Whether two or 20 students, a minimum number of students is likely to be needed to keep a club viable. It would be useful to have an idea of what this number is for your club. Table 5.4 lists some potential issues to do with falling membership and suggests

Table 5.4 Potential STEM club membership issues

Issue	Suggested strategies
After a few sessions numbers start to drop	Try to find out why. Ask non-attenders or email them a very short questionnaire
	If the club does not cater for the diversity of members, they may leave. Adjust the programme to be more or less challenging or contain a greater variety of activities
	If the club does not allow equal opportunities, e.g. those who can build circuit boards push out those who can't, training, mentoring or partnership work might address this
Other school activities or commitments take priority	There may be little that you can do apart from making the club as attractive and welcoming as possible
	Students often have several options to choose from. Making the outcomes clear, along with the benefits, may persuade some students to choose your club over others, e.g. a presentation at a STEM fair or an award to add to their CV
Few from minority groups attend	Find out what these would like to do by sending out questionnaires
	Find activities or challenges that appeal to particular groups
	Read the STEM Equality and Diversity Toolkit (see Chapter 9). Try out some of the suggestions
Attendance declines through the year	Keep a register to monitor attendance
	Look for any patterns in non-attendance
	Keep notes of what went well/what did not work so well
	Ask for brief feedback at the end of sessions
Some students mention they may not continue to attend	Find out why and address the issue if possible. If it is something that cannot be fixed, then do not take it personally
	Consider entering one or more competitions, so club members have an ongoing project to work on rather than one-off activities. This promotes teamwork and project management. If club members know they have a deadline to meet and can see their project improving each session, they should feel needed
	Choose projects that arouse students' curiosity. Have a practical that won't give results until next week, so that they are keen to come back and find out what happened
	Have fun during the sessions

possible strategies to address these, with the aim of keeping membership above the minimum sustainable number.

Money

Most schools have small budgets for running extracurricular clubs, but these won't be endless and clubs that require lots of consumable materials may find that finances start to become an issue.

Costing out activities at the start of a programme is useful, but not always practical as numbers of students change and projects may take different directions.

Keep records of outgoings and any income. Students could do this, with a member of staff acting as auditor. Chapter 8 has ideas about funding STEM clubs.

Embedding sustainability

As well as being sustainable, in the sense of viable, STEM clubs could model good practice in sustainability. The Ofsted (2008) report on schools and sustainability stated that 'the Government wants all schools to become "sustainable schools" by 2020' but that 'most of the schools visited had limited knowledge of sustainability'.

A school will only become a properly 'sustainable school' if sustainability is embedded throughout the school, extracurricular clubs included. So, encourage club members to follow best practices, as laid down by the school, or by leading the way.

- Recycle materials.
- Use recycled materials if possible.
- Don't use materials unless necessary.
- Don't use more materials than necessary.
- Make the most of any materials, e.g. cutting out wisely to make the most of a fabric or piece of aluminium.
- Consider alternative materials that may be more sustainable.
- Have a club representative on the school's council or 'green team' or body that is responsible for promoting sustainability.
- Encourage projects that investigate aspects of sustainability.

In this way, the club could contribute towards whole school sustainability, including Eco-school status.

Chapter 6

Encouraging STEM careers

By the end of this chapter, you will know:

* the important role of teachers in raising awareness of the range of jobs available from studying STEM subjects
* where teachers, students and parents can get current information about STEM careers, education and training routes
* how information about STEM careers education can be promoted in schools.

Careers in STEM, careers from STEM

Everyone in the developed world uses STEM skills every day of their lives. Our society's dependence on sophisticated transport systems, energy supplies and communications and information technology means that the range of jobs drawing on STEM skills has increased dramatically. Careers options for young people leaving full-time education are markedly different generation by generation. This makes it really important that all learners have access to appropriate courses to ensure development of deep and broad STEM literacy skills. Such skills will enable them to engage with, and exploit, new technologies as they appear.

The UK Commission for Employment and Skills (UKCES) defined STEM skills as skills supporting scientific enquiry and research, and the growth of these disciplines, including:

* data analysis and interpretation
* research and experimental design
* testing hypotheses
* analysis and problem-solving
* technical skills.

In its briefing paper 'The supply of and demand for high-level STEM skills', UKCES predicted that around 58 per cent of new jobs expected to appear in the UK between 2007 and 2017 will require employees with STEM skills. This throws the onus on to schools to provide the range of experiences for students that will help them become useful to employers as well as successful adults (UKCES 2011).

Arguments for educating our young people to become STEM-literate citizens were presented in Chapter 1. Here we concentrate on ways of helping them appreciate the diverse range of careers drawing on different levels of functional literacy in STEM subjects.

We use 'STEM careers' to include:

- careers specialising in one or more of the STEM subjects (careers in STEM)
- careers needing good STEM skills (careers from STEM), such as the numeracy skills required by interior decorators or the scientific knowledge and understanding required by physiotherapists.

In the UK, there are different styles of STEM courses for students in their final years of secondary education, depending on prior academic attainment and career intentions. Students aspiring to careers in STEM are encouraged to build a strong suite of academic STEM qualifications by selecting courses offering breadth and depth. Students planning to enter careers requiring STEM as 'supporting' subjects have the option of studying less intense STEM courses.

Giving quality advice to students about STEM careers is a challenge. According to Yvonne Baker, Chief Executive of Myscience:

> Anyone who has worked in the scientific industries knows how complex it is to explain exactly what their job entails. The term 'engineer' or 'scientist' doesn't even begin to describe the enormous range of opportunities that are available to those with scientific qualifications from school or university – qualifications which, it is estimated, deliver an uplift for STEM graduates of £250k in earnings over their lifetime.
>
> (Baker 2013)

The government recommends that schools offer practical careers advice, including engagement with local employers and other insights into the world of work (Public Policy Exchange Symposium 2013). Teachers of STEM subjects in the UK are fortunate as free support is available to contact STEM specialists. These can visit schools and act as role models or learning mentors through the established STEM ambassador programme.

Baker's 2013 statement in the UK about the earning potential of employees with STEM competencies and skills matches similar financial benefits reported from the USA, where employees in STEM occupations typically have higher average salaries than other workers. In 2010, US STEM workers earned 26 per cent more than non-STEM workers, even after accounting for other factors that affected pay (US Department of Commerce, Economics and Statistics Administration 2011a).

Helping students explore career options is a huge responsibility and the good news is that teachers are not expected to know all the answers. They are, however, expected to be able to contribute to the process of Careers Education, Information, Advice and Guidance (CEIAG) by signposting opportunities, and the next sections look at ways to do this.

Sources of career information and advice

Young people constantly receive messages about the roles of adults in society. At every stage in education they will have a view of the 'world of work' shaped by an accumulation of personal experiences of the role models in their immediate lives: parents and family, neighbours, teachers and images portrayed by the media.

Evidence from a survey conducted on behalf of the UK Equal Opportunities Commission suggests that career aspirations may strongly mirror the cultural and societal environments in which students grow up, and that this may be a factor in the underrepresentation of lower socioeconomic groups in certain careers. Similar arguments may explain the low take-up of STEM careers in physical science areas by girls (Equal Opportunities Commission 2005; Francis *et al.* 2005).

The questions:

> How can you dream of being an engineer if you don't know what one is?

> If you have never seen, never heard, a women inventing something, fixing something, will girls dream about doing that job when older?

> (Munn 2011)

are echoed in the findings of a 3-year longitudinal student survey conducted as part of the STEM Cohesion Programme evaluation (National Foundation for Educational Research 2011). The majority of students identified 'parents and relatives' as their main source of STEM careers information, closely followed by teachers. Over a third of students in the survey reported getting careers information from Careers or Personal, Social and Health Education lessons, leaflets or booklets or from events in school involving visiting STEM professionals.

In follow-up interviews, students said that they would have liked more direct reference to STEM careers in lessons:

> If they showed you more about what jobs or careers could come from certain subjects, like Maths, there would be more interest in them.

> I want to be able to say to someone 'I enjoy this aspect of Biology so how would I go about getting a job where I can use that aspect?'

Ideas for broadening students' exposure to possible careers and suggestions for challenging stereotypes are discussed later in this chapter.

CEIAG

Used widely in education, the term 'CEIAG' represents Careers Education, Information, Advice and Guidance. This includes:

- careers signposting within lessons
- extracurricular activities raising students' awareness of the range of careers, i.e. careers education and information
- formal careers advice and guidance, the responsibility of careers information professionals.

Careers *education* provides comprehensive packages allowing young people to make informed choices about career pathways. It should ensure that they know the necessary steps in taking courses and achieving qualifications to follow career routes.

Usually, careers education is provided through the collaboration of specialists. These include subject teachers, school staff trained to deliver careers advice and often careers guidance counsellors contracted by the school to provide additional expertise.

There is no longer central funding for independent careers guidance counsellors to work in schools in England. Costs are now passed on to individual schools. The political argument for the change was that it moved from a 'one size fits all' provision to empowering school managers to design and commission the most appropriate careers education packages for their students. It is too soon to assess the impact of these funding changes.

Subject specialists such as STEM teachers are expected to signpost links from the curriculum areas they are teaching to possible careers. This helps supply *information* about the existence of a range of STEM careers beyond the ones students may already know about and may also provide *advice* about how students could find out more about such careers.

The STEM Programme Report (2006) identified improvement of the quality of advice and guidance for students, teachers and parents about STEM careers as a priority area, resulting in a number of intervention projects.

Section 29 of the Education Act, 2011, placed schools under a duty to secure access to independent careers guidance for their pupils in school years 9–11 (ages 13–16). From September 2013 this requirement is extended to years 8–13 (ages 12–19 years). The Act specifies that guidance 'must be presented in an impartial manner and include information on the full range of post-16 education or training options, including Apprenticeships'.

> Schools should consider a range of wider careers activities such as engagement with local employers and work-based education and training providers to offer all young people insights into the world of work, and with local colleges and universities for first-hand experience of further and higher education. Schools are free to determine the most appropriate forms of engagement but might consider mentoring, workplace visits, work experience, work shadowing, enterprise clubs, employer talks and links with local higher education institutions.
>
> (Department for Education 2013b)

One difficulty of providing good CEIAG is the relative lack of experience of contemporary STEM careers by adults providing this service. Recognising the major role that teachers play in shaping students' career aspirations, STEM stakeholders such as major STEM employers, professional associations and universities aim to provide teachers with information about routes in education and training.

In 2011, EngineeringUK canvassed primary and secondary teachers to find out more about their preferred means of extending their knowledge of STEM careers and what sources of information they recommended to their students. Almost 90 per cent of teachers indicated preference for the internet, with 98 per cent reporting that they would recommend internet resources for students. Around half the teachers mentioned leaflets and posters, suggesting these are still valued, particularly for display in classrooms and noticeboards (Engineering UK 2011a).

One legacy of the STEM Cohesion Programme is the Future Morph portal for STEM careers information. This is an excellent 'first stop' for teachers, parents and young people, with new information, careers profiles and links to reliable websites added regularly.

Timing of STEM CEIAG

In the past, some schools provided careers advice in the months, or the academic year, before students left school or before selecting options from subject combinations. This 'just in time' approach to providing careers advice is now regarded as too little, too late.

Evidence indicates that young people make career decisions or close their minds to certain careers at an early age, based on the informal accumulation of information from the social and cultural environment in which they grow up (University of Warwick 2009; Wellcome Trust 2010; Munn 2011; Ofsted 2011c). It is now considered important that schools contribute to students' awareness of careers options as early as possible.

A survey conducted for the Royal Society questioned over 1,000 STEM professionals to find out when they had made decisions about their chosen careers. Over a quarter of respondents admitted to thinking about a STEM career before the age of 11, with a further third making decisions between the ages of 12 and 14 years (Royal Society 2006).

The ASPIRES project, based at King's College London, explored influences on career aspirations by following groups of students aged 9–13 years (Archer *et al.* 2012). Started in 2009, this 4-year project investigated effects of gender, class, ethnicity, family life and school Science and Maths experiences on students' careers aspirations. The final report is due towards the end of 2013 but interim reports, available from the project website, provide evidence and convincing arguments for early careers intervention. They also provide suggestions for teachers about useful strategies, some of which are explored later in this chapter.

Recognising the importance of their role in helping shape views about future careers, a growing number of primary schools, serving students from ages 4 to 11, in the UK are organising 'Aspirations' days (not directly related to the ASPIRES project, just sharing a common message about their purpose). A typical Aspiration event involves adults from diverse businesses and careers contributing to a 'market-place' with artefacts, photos of themselves or colleagues at their place of work presenting a picture of what they do during a working day. Students and parents are encouraged to approach the exhibitors to find out what is involved in particular jobs.

The principle of introducing information about different jobs in STEM through case studies and by giving young people access to role models was highlighted in the *Lengthening Ladders, Shortening Snakes* report (University of Warwick 2009). Based on a longitudinal study of embedding STEM careers information in the early years of secondary education (11–14 years), the report pointed out that, whilst employers and higher education institutes strongly value 'STEM skills', an overemphasis on this term in isolation from 'real examples' can backfire. Students respond better to holistic, humanist images of STEM in the workplace.

Signposting STEM careers

Common messages from research, referred to previously, suggest that early and regular exposure to STEM careers information encourages more young people to explore careers in, or based on, STEM.

Formal events, such as careers fairs, are valuable for showing students how curriculum subjects relate to the world of work, but cannot give comprehensive overviews of career opportunities in specific areas. Some schools compensate by tapping into the resources and support offered by STEMNET to operate bespoke STEM careers events. As parents' understanding of career options can be a determining factor, the most successful careers events include opportunities for parents as well as students.

A creative approach to providing timely careers information is given in Case Study 6.1.

CASE STUDY 6.1   Early signposting of careers opportunities

The UK schools involved were part of a tripartite education system with primary, middle and high schools serving the local communities. Individual high schools at the top of this education pyramid had very low numbers of students, arriving from the middle schools, planning to follow the Triple Science route, i.e. to study separate Biology, Physics and Chemistry GCSE courses – the recommended choice for students aspiring to follow careers in STEM.

Investigation showed that many students decided about careers and courses of study in the middle schools. Traditionally little careers signposting had taken place with these middle school students, aged 9–13 years old. The split in locations between middle and secondary schools meant that older students studying STEM subjects were not available as role models.

In an ambitious intervention, the local authority Science advisor set up a small working party, including school staff and the local STEMNET contract holder, to plan a STEM careers fair open to all final-year students at local middle schools. A separate session was available at the end of the day for families, i.e. parents and offspring together, to give students the chance to show parents what interested them. This helped build on initial interest and opened new horizons.

The impact was virtually instant: numbers of students applying to follow Triple Science programmes in the high schools increased. Funding did not allow further STEM careers fairs, but teachers, inspired by the impact of the original event, devised careers information events within their middle schools in following years.

By using case studies, featuring STEM role models, from Future Morph and other websites, and by thinking about students' prior experiences of STEM, teachers could create a brief for visitors to their schools. The Briefing Pack for STEM Careers Ambassadors (see end of chapter) has pre-visit checklists that could be adapted to get the most out of careers events.

Other careers events used successfully by schools include hosting 'STEM Experience' events, such as the free Tomorrow's Engineers road show or other STEM road shows (see below). Paid events could also be considered, where organisations bring a series of workshops to school for a day, repeating sessions several times over the day so many students access the experiences.

Some professional institutions will bring workshops to individual schools; others will approach local members to try to find someone able to support a careers event. Availability of support varies with the amount of funding allocated by the institutions to schools' outreach annually. Events involving large numbers of students are generally considered to be a more cost-effective use of limited resources, so consider opening up careers events to other local schools to increase the audience size and to make the outreach more attractive for potential contributors.

With such a range of potential outreach activities to consider, a good place to start researching what is available within a locality in the UK is to use the online STEM Directories or approach the local STEMNET contract holder who can offer free advice.

Another major, and potentially more potent, way of providing STEM careers information is to integrate activities into the curriculum to provide careers signposting. This can also offer the possibility of follow-up discussions of STEM careers and the opportunity to invite STEM ambassadors to contribute to parts of lessons. Holman and Finegold (2010), in

Table 6.1 Science lessons, for students aged 12 years, integrating careers information

Lesson	Career integration
1	School nurse invited to contribute to initial theory of Biology behind *in vitro* fertilisation (IVF)
2	Students role-play perspectives of would-be parents, counsellors and medical team involved in IVF; class discuss the range of STEM jobs necessary to enable the couple to conceive a baby via IVF
3	Groups research professions involved in IVF, producing a poster to share findings

their STEM Careers Review, recommend that STEM teachers should take appropriate opportunities to embed 'elements of STEM careers awareness to contextualise their teaching and help bring their subject to life'. They also recommend integrating careers information into lessons so it appears seamless to students, rather than 'bolted on'.

Most providers of careers information for the educational market are balanced in terms of encouraging boys and girls to consider STEM roles. Many have examples of successful employees in 'non-traditional' roles to support teachers in tackling career stereotyping. However, if students carry out their own research into STEM jobs, they may visit websites, less carefully monitored, so it is a good idea to encourage students to use portals such as Future Morph as starting points for searches. The next section looks at tackling career stereotyping in greater detail.

Although it takes time to alter lessons or schemes of work to incorporate career signposting, it does not necessarily mean that remaining lessons in the topic will be compromised to 'make up for time lost doing the careers lesson'. With the careers element of the work integrated into the learning, the pace of an overall scheme of work can be maintained.

Examples of series of lessons that integrate careers information are available to download from the National STEM Centre elibrary.

The example in Table 6.1 illustrates the ease with which 'invisible' STEM jobs can be brought to the attention of students and provide a range of alternative career options in the field of medicine when otherwise they might only think of the media-popularised roles of doctors, nurses and paramedics.

It is not suggested that this depth of careers exploration takes place for every topic, but by identifying one or two opportunities per STEM subject per term, students will be exposed to many applications of STEM. These strategies, in conjunction with other promotional STEM activities in schools, are associated with improved interest in STEM careers in schools where they have been trialled.

Tackling stereotypes

It is known (e.g. via the 2009–2013 ASPIRES project) that by the age of 10 or 11, many UK students lose interest in STEM careers. In the ASPIRES study over 70 per cent of students agreed that they were interested in Science and recognised that 'scientists made a difference to the world', but less than a third expressed an interest in 'having a job using Science' and less than 20 per cent wanted 'to become scientists'.

Why do students find careers in STEM relatively unattractive? Is it because of strong competition from other careers? Or are they rejecting Science and Engineering because of stereotyped images of STEM professionals that do not fit with future aspirations?

Table 6.2 Views of young people aged 14–15 about non-traditional jobs

Question	Positive responses (%)	
	Boys	Girls
Would you be concerned about getting teased if you took up a non-traditional job?	48	12
Have you any concerns about how you might be treated if you were working in a non-traditional job?	45	63
If your parents disapproved of you taking up a non-traditional job, would this put you off?	9	20

One of the major barriers to follow careers in non-traditional areas is the difficulty in finding correct information. Sometimes older generations have impressions of job roles that are no longer valid. For example, modern production lines generally include far less manual labour, with many repetitive jobs being carried out mechanically. Thus the technical skills of the workforce exceed those of previous workers making similar products. Parents, grandparents and other older adults having outdated or incomplete pictures about present and future prospects in the STEM world are not helpful, especially when many new opportunities become available with each wave of scientific and technological development.

Phrases like: 'that's a man's job' and 'that is too dirty/difficult/dangerous for a woman' are banned from the world of employment and recruitment through legislation, but such opinions survive in pockets of society, influencing some students considering their future. Some young people showing an interest in pursuing further education or training in a 'non-traditional' area may have to defend their decision.

Work carried out on behalf of the Equal Opportunities Commission (2005) asked over 1,800 young people (aged 14 and 15) their views about non-traditional jobs. Table 6.2 shows some of the results.

Gender stereotypes

Around three decades since the first Women into Science and Engineering (WISE) initiatives in the UK attempted to break down stereotypes and promote equal participation in STEM careers for women, we are still looking at considerable gender imbalances in the workforce.

Female participation in STEM decreases as soon as it stops being a core curriculum subject. At age 16 in England, female participation is approximately 50 per cent; by age 18 this proportion drops to 45 per cent. These overall statistics, provided by the WISE Project, provided in report by UKRC in 2010, hide great variations across the STEM subjects, as Figure 6.1 shows.

The decline in the number of girls studying STEM subjects continues at higher education level, with only about one-third of STEM undergraduates being female. After graduation, the 'leaky pipe' effect continues, with around 12 per cent of the STEM workforce in England being female (Engineering UK 2011b).

In 2007, the European Labour Force Survey reported on the proportion of female engineers working in the 28 European states. The UK came 28/28, with just 8.7 per cent of its engineering workforce being female. Latvia was top, with 30 per cent of its engineers being female (European Labour Force Survey 2007).

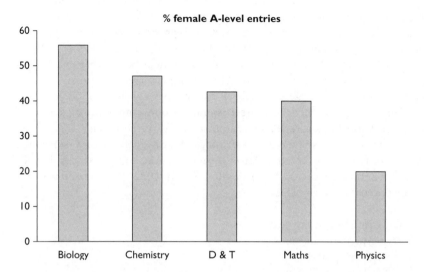

% female A-level entries

Figure 6.1 Percentage of A-level (UK exam at age 17–18) entries in STEM subjects in the UK taken by girls, summer 2012.

It has been estimated that removing barriers to women working in occupations traditionally done by men and increasing women's participation in the UK's labour market could be worth £15–23 billion or 1.3–2.0 per cent of the gross domestic product (Engineering UK 2011b).

The situation in the USA is only slightly better than in the UK. Despite more American females earning bachelor degrees than males, only 14 per cent of engineering graduates in 2010 were female (US Congress Joint Economic Committee 2012) and only 27 per cent of the Computer Science and Maths employment positions in the USA were held by women (US Department of Commerce, Economics and Statistics Administration 2011b).

A survey in the UK suggested that gender stereotyping was a major contributing factor in students' career choices. This survey reported that girls, from a very young age, had formed an understanding of conventions about 'girls' jobs' and 'boys' jobs'. In cases where girls had selected unconventional subject choices or career pathways, it was often the result of personal experiences countering the stereotypes (Ofsted 2011c).

The same survey looked in detail at four schools where older girls were identified as showing particular interest in STEM. These schools reported delivering STEM enrichment activities involving teachers, students, outside agencies and local companies. Typically the activities were a mixture of projects and presentations, competitions and design challenges to enrich students' experiences. Data collected by the schools indicated a higher percentage of girls than boys were involved in the activities. The girls interviewed said that they enjoyed their engagement in novel and challenging activities and that meeting the female role models had inspired and encouraged them.

Further evidence of positive experiences enjoyed by girls, through applying STEM knowledge and skills in competitions, is provided by the proportion of female finalists in major STEM competitions and challenges across the UK. See, for example, the British Science Association, CREST Awards, Case studies web page with information about past finalists of the Young Scientist and Young Engineer of the Year competitions.

Teachers everywhere could provide female students with access to similar engaging and inspirational experiences by setting up their own enrichment programmes of talks and visits. Advice about getting started and where to get ideas for enrichment activities is provided in Chapters 3–5.

Many of the skills the girls reported enjoying in their STEM enrichment time (Ofsted 2011c) are ones that form foundations for successful entrepreneurship. Perhaps we should be pointing this out more and encouraging girls to broaden their career options.

Current employment statistics suggest that entrepreneurship is a growing option for both genders but 'becoming an entrepreneur' is a career aspiration more commonly suggested by boys than by girls. The Global Entrepreneurship Monitor (GEM) project is an annual assessment of entrepreneurial activity, aspirations and attitudes of individuals across a wide range of countries. A team of researchers based at Aston Business School collect the UK data for the project and in 2012 it was reported (Aston Business School 2012) that over 20 per cent of the working-age population in the UK:

- expected to start a business in the next 3 years
- were actively trying to start a business
- were running their own business.

Although men are responsible for twice as many new start-up companies in the UK annually, a report prepared from GEM statistics for the UK states that:

> women-owned firms outperform those owned by their male counterparts, when firm characteristics are controlled for (i.e. business age, sector and size) as well as the attributes of the individual (i.e. education, age and income).
>
> (RBS Group 2012)

Making a point of praising all students for the quality of their work is always good, but taking time to make explicit how much those qualities are appreciated in the world of work is particularly important for self-esteem and ultimately for career decisions. Adolescent girls in particular need a lot of personal conviction, and external reassurance, as well as internal commitment, to select non-traditional careers. Receiving positive feedback about their capacity to tackle typical tasks required for success in a STEM career could be just the extra reassurance needed to persuade some girls to go against stereotypes and continue in STEM education or training after school.

There are some good examples of positive intervention available from the Girls into Engineering project (see end of chapter).

Black and minority ethnic (BME) and other minority groups

A whole range of cultural, socioeconomic and personal influences affects students' decisions about career aspirations, education and training pathways. One factor is students' own assessment of their ability to progress successfully in the subject(s) concerned. Evidence shows that even achieving good examination results at age 16 does not give the majority sufficient interest or confidence about their ability in STEM subjects to study them at a higher level (Wellcome Trust 2010).

Analysis of national examination results (Joint Council for Qualifications 2012b) suggests that students' concerns about their ability are largely unfounded. This adds weight to arguments put forward earlier for STEM teachers to promote careers options and pathways in an integrated way across the STEM curriculum so that students are better informed well before they have to make decisions about future study or training.

Statistics about examination performance at age 16 (Joint Council for Qualifications 2012b) suggest that academic achievement varies across socioeconomic and cultural groups, possibly providing an indication of academic motivation but certainly having an impact on options for continued study or level of entry into the workforce. Significantly, in all combinations of factors reported in the Department for Education statistics for GCSE examinations in the summer of 2012 in England, girls outperformed boys (Department for Education 2013c).

There is also evidence to suggest that students from different ethnic groups have varying levels of performance, although the categories used in the reports (Wellcome Trust 2010) are so broad (for example, the category 'Asian background' encompasses a huge number of countries, some with quite contrasting cultures) that the reported trends have to be treated with caution. Nevertheless, they offer important points for teachers and careers specialists to consider when encouraging students from different ethnic backgrounds to consider the range of STEM options.

Some key facts from the 2012 Department for Education statistics for examination results in England (Department for Education 2013), based on the average percentages of students gaining at least 5 A*–C grades in the GCSE examinations, including Mathematics and English are as follows.

- Pupils of any white background achieved broadly in line with the national level.
- Pupils of any black background on average achieved below the national level – a gap of 3.8 percentage points. The good news is that this gap has been narrowing year on year, halving in the period 2007–2012.
- Pupils from Asian backgrounds performed above the national level, a gap of 3.6 percentage points. In this case, the gap has widened slightly in the period 2007–2012.
- Chinese pupils are the highest-attaining ethnic group. The attainment gap between Chinese pupils and the national level was a whopping 20.4 percentage points in 2012.

Evidence of the participation of BME employees in the STEM workforce tends to be reported sector by sector, so is difficult to collate, but figures for university courses are collected centrally and provide some encouraging statistics:

- In 2006–2007, among UK-domiciled students, similar proportions of white women and BME women obtained undergraduate (34.8 and 35.8 per cent respectively) and postgraduate qualifications (39.8 and 38.5 per cent respectively) in STEM.
- In 2008, BME women were more likely to work in Science, Engineering and Technology (SET) occupations than white women: 8.2 per cent of all BME working women compared to 5.1 per cent of all white working women.
- In recent years the participation of BME women in SET occupations has been increasing at a faster rate than the participation of white women (UKRC 2010).

Although at just over one-third of the undergraduate student population in STEM subjects women are still hugely underrepresented, the pattern is not exacerbated across ethnic groups. In this respect it appears as though the situation in the UK is slightly better than that in the USA where:

> Of particular concern are the persistent STEM participation and achievement gaps across different demographic groups. In particular, women are less likely than men to pursue degrees in STEM, and black and Hispanic students are less likely than white students.
>
> (US Congress Joint Economic Committee 2012)

Teachers can draw on the improving statistics for successful participation in STEM areas to encourage their students in this direction. A very useful resource for teachers is the 'toolkit' developed through the London Engineering Project and distributed as the STEM Subject Choice and Careers Online Equality and Diversity Toolkit (see Chapter 9). STEMNET is another good source of support across the UK through its STEM ambassadors programme, although it cannot guarantee the availability of an ambassador from specific ethnic groups. STEMNET's local contract holders work closely with schools and ensure visiting ambassadors work with schools to promote STEM careers in a positive way to all students.

Activities to help signpost STEM careers

Most teachers of STEM subjects have their personal experience of STEM careers 'frozen in time' at the point when they chose to work in education and so need to update their knowledge and understanding of the changing commercial and industrial applications associated with their subject continuously.

The past decade has seen considerable investment by STEM stakeholders to support efforts by schools to promote STEM careers to both learners and their parents. Careers resources have been distributed to schools, media campaigns commissioned and support such as sponsored professional development training for STEM teachers and careers advisors has been made available.

A major government involvement in STEM careers promotion happened during 2008–2009 with advertising aimed at students and their families and the launch of STEM careers information and signposting websites, such as Future Morph and its partner website, Maths Careers. Both are arranged to accommodate interests of different ages of visitors to the sites, with areas for teachers and other adults. Complementing these websites is the growing range of careers resources available to browse and download from the National STEM Centre elibrary.

An important asset, available to all schools, is often overlooked. A survey of some schools in England showed that no school had systematic records of the employment of former students. Anecdotes of individual cases were uncovered where former students returned to support the careers education programme, but there was no evidence of schools asking former students 'what could we have done better to support your career development?' (Ofsted 2011c).

Good links with STEM alumni gives schools access to rich supplies of role models. The immediacy of some alumni to the school students, with some even still having siblings in the school, brings careers information and signposting to life better than any leaflet or video. Past students, and perhaps through them, more senior STEM figures from employers or universities could be invited to contribute to curriculum topics as well as careers events. Building up a register of past students is a long-term project, but the rewards would justify the effort.

Working with parents and carers

Parents, carers, extended families and friends have huge formative influences on young people and contribute to students' views about their future roles in life, including possible careers.

A survey exploring parents' and carers' knowledge of, and attitudes towards, careers in Engineering concluded that there was generally little awareness of different types of Engineering. A bias towards service-orientated industries such as banking and law was identified in many responses, suggesting that employment in 'mainstream' STEM was promoted less in the households surveyed. As a result, it was recommended that support with careers information, advice and guidance should be targeted to the parents/carers of children at primary school and upwards as well as the young people themselves (Engineering UK 2011c).

One way to raise parents' knowledge about STEM careers is to have these well represented at careers information events. The STEM careers web portals listed at the end of the chapter are good sources of information and have links to up-to-date careers resources that can be used in information booklets. Some of the careers videos featuring applications of STEM in the workplace (some quite unusual or unexpected workplaces!) could be downloaded and played on a loop on a display screen where parents are gathering during careers events, so adding to the opportunity to represent many different aspects of STEM.

STEM ambassadors are another valuable source of careers information and can talk from personal experience about working in STEM. Some STEM ambassadors attend additional training to be better prepared to promote STEM careers and answer questions about required qualifications and training from students and parents.

As pointed out by the EngineeringUK report, not only are many parents poorly informed about the full range of careers options, they appear to be attracted to the sort of service careers which are associated, in the media at least, with lucrative salaries. If these parents were fully informed about the financial benefits associated with STEM careers, then it is possible that their views about careers options would be more impartial or even biased in the direction of STEM.

The UK government prepares quarterly employment statistics, referred to as the 'UK Labour Force Survey data'. Analyses of the data have been used to quantify the financial benefits of graduate employment in different employment sectors, compared to the earnings of peers with similar qualifications at age 18, who chose to enter the workforce instead of going to university. The comparisons look at average earnings in each sector for people of different ages and also at cumulative lifetime earnings. When comparing average initial salaries, STEM careers in Medicine, Dentistry, Maths and Computer Science all exceed or compare very favourably with the high salaries associated with finance and law, with Veterinary Science, 'subjects allied to Medicine', Engineering and Education all within 10 per cent of the top salaries (Department for Business, Innovation and Skills 2011).

Another study, based on the same statistics, suggests that whilst starting salaries were higher in Law, Economics and Management (LEM), in terms of lifetime salaries, STEM graduates accumulated at least as much income as those in the LEM sector (Walker and Zhu 2011).

Many other STEM careers, whilst not competing directly on income with the ones already listed, lead to higher than average graduate salaries and suggest good financial returns on the time and money invested in the additional studying. The statistics on which these figures are based (Department for Business, Innovation and Skills 2011) take into account the costs of university fees and living expenses whilst studying, so are also useful to have available if students and parents bring up concerns about student financing.

Arguments about financial and lifestyle benefits of STEM careers are helpful as part of a range of approaches to promote STEM careers, but on their own are unlikely to 'hook' young people, many of whom tend to be swayed by promises of immediate financial gains offered by law and other non-STEM careers. However if parents are well informed about these issues and encouraged to discuss careers with their children, this will support the work in schools by teachers and careers staff to ensure that young people make fully informed career choices.

Websites such as Future Morph maintain regular updates of case studies of people working in a range of STEM careers and many include information about typical salaries. As suggested earlier, case studies, providing insight into the different aspects of the work involved in individual careers, provide important and influential contributions to CEIAG activities.

Sources of STEM careers information

Aspires Project: www.kcl.ac.uk/sspp/departments/education/research/aspires/aims.aspx

Briefing Pack for STEM Careers Ambassadors, Department for Education (2009) http://www.nationalstemcentre.org.uk/elibrary/resource/1619/briefing-pack-for-stem-careers-ambassadors

Future Morph: www.futuremorph.org

Girls into Engineering: http://www.stemcymru.org.uk/project-strands/girls-into-engineering/

Maths Careers: http://www.mathscareers.org.uk

National STEM Centre elibrary: http://www.nationalstemcentre.org.uk/elibrary/careers/

Research Councils UK. Series of careers in research case studies: http://www.rcuk.ac.uk/ResearchCareers/percase/Pages/home.aspx

Science and Maths Net: www.scienceandmaths.net

Secondary STEM Roadshows: http://www.sentinus.co.uk/product.php?id=10

STEM Careers Database – embed a customisable Careers 'widget' on your own website with the coding available from the National STEM Centre http://www.nationalstemcentre.org.uk/stem-in-context/careers-database

STEMNET: www.stemnet.org.uk

The Hidden Science Map: http://www.hiddensciencemap.org/resources/teachers

WISE: www.wisecampaign.org.uk/education/useful-links

Chapter 7

Health, safety and legal issues

What you can and can't do

By the end of this chapter, you will have an awareness of:

- potential health and safety issues associated with running STEM activities
- legal aspects relevant to running STEM activities in and out of the classroom
- recommended best practice.

Notes

1   Guidance given in this chapter is for England unless otherwise stated. If you are working in another country you need to find out what regulations apply.
2   Although information was correct at the time of writing, legislation does change so it is important to check for updates.

Don't let 'red tape' stop you from running exciting sessions, events or visits for students. Rules and regulations are there to keep you, your students and others safe. Avoidance of any activity involving hazards would make much practical work impossible and diminish the education and experiences of your students.

This chapter aims to raise awareness of what can and cannot be done. Much more can be done than most people think; consider just a few of the common misconceptions addressed in Table 7.1. Perhaps the main thing, with any new activity, is to use a good dash of common sense and if you don't know something, find out.

> Children should be able to experience a wide range of activities. Health and safety measures should help them to do this safely, not stop them. It is important that children learn to understand and manage the risks that are a normal part of life.
>
> Common sense should be used in assessing and managing the risks of any activity. Health and safety procedures should always be proportionate to the risks of an activity. Staff should be given the training they need so they can keep themselves and children safe and manage risks effectively.
>
> (Department for Education 2012b)

Overall responsibility for health and safety lies with the employer. Who the employer is will depend on the category of school (Health and Safety Executive 2011a).

This chapter explains some of what you need to know about health, safety and legal issues related to running STEM activities and suggests where to find further information.

Table 7.1 Some misconceptions: what can and can't be done in and out of STEM lessons

Misconception	Explanation
Eyes, such as cow's eyes, cannot be dissected in school	Eyes can be dissected, as can other materials from butchers or abattoirs. Washing hands after dissection reduces risk of oral infection. Some students prefer not to handle any material from pigs due to religious/cultural beliefs
	The Biotechnology and Biological Sciences Research Council (BBSRC) has produced a useful guide about eyes that includes advice about dissecting eyes, for 14–18-year-olds (see Chapter 9)
Human cheek cell and blood sampling is no longer allowed in schools	Human fluids may be used in schools subject to agreement from the appropriate local authority or governing body and suitable risk assessments
	Using sterile, soft cotton buds for cheek sampling and safe disposal of the used bud makes cheek cell sampling acceptable
	Human blood sampling is allowed as long as an appropriate risk assessment is carried out. It is sensible to reserve this activity for responsible students, perhaps 16+ and under controlled conditions. Some colleges and schools regularly use human blood in lab practicals
	CLEAPSS and the Association for Science Education (2001) have published procedures for taking blood samples safely
Setting off fireworks and smoke bombs is not acceptable on school grounds	From a safety point of view, there is no objection to setting off commercially available fireworks or smoke bombs on the school field as part of a lesson or STEM club
	A full risk assessment (for guidance, see CLEAPSS 2008) should be written and it would be sensible to give the Head and other staff advance notice of the proposed activity
Machines, such as sanders, polishers and grinders, that do not stop quickly need braking devices	There appears to be no need for this: overzealous safety reports may be responsible for this misconception about Design & Technology equipment
Design & Technology classes should have a maximum of 20 students	This is false, apart from Scotland. The Department for Education gives no recommendations on class size
	The established convention that Design & Technology classes have a maximum of 20 is no more than a convention in England and Wales; it has no legal basis outside Scotland (where classes in all practical subjects are restricted to a maximum of 20 pupils) and Northern Ireland. However, it does seem a sensible recommendation

Source of information: mainly from CLEAPSS website.

Misconceptions about what you can/can't do

It is difficult to measure the impact of practical work, including trips out of school (Abrahams and Millar 2008; Dohn 2011; Giffould 2011; see Chapter 3) but it is generally accepted that practical activities have positive effects on students' attitudes (Royal Society of Chemistry 2007; Wellcome Trust 2012). Despite that, the Royal Society of Chemistry (RSC) (2007) noted that: 'exciting hands-on work in schools seems to be on the decline. Health and safety restrictions are often quoted as a barrier to exciting practical work.'

In 2005, the RSC commissioned the Consortium of Local Education Authorities for the Provision of Science Services (CLEAPSS) (Box 7.1) to investigate the presumption that certain experiments or chemicals are banned, thus perhaps preventing some exciting practical work (Royal Society of Chemistry 2007). Questionnaires were sent to over 1,500 secondary schools in the UK and to education officers in all the education authorities. The findings showed that many misconceptions existed about the types of chemicals and activities that are banned and that, in some cases, learning and teaching were inhibited by unjustified concerns about health and safety.

Box 7.1 CLEAPSS

The name CLEAPSS is now a trademark, not an acronym. This subscription advisory service provides support for Science and Technology in local authorities and schools, from nursery through to 16–19 education.

CLEAPSS serves teachers, head teachers, teacher trainers, technicians, Science advisors/inspectors/consultants, health and safety advisors and school governors. It has around 2,000 associate members, including independent schools, overseas institutions, field centres, museums and curriculum developers.

CLEAPSS covers:

- health and safety, including model risk assessments
- chemicals, living organisms, equipment
- sources of resources
- Science and Design & Technology laboratory design, facilities and fittings
- technicians and their jobs.

CLEAPSS provides:

- newsletters for primary and secondary schools each term
- a wide range of free publications
- model and special risk assessments
- 'Haz' cards and the latest information on hazard warning symbols
- training courses for technicians, teachers and local authority officers
- a telephone helpline (01895 251 496)
- a monitoring service, e.g. for mercury spills
- evaluations of equipment
- advice on repairs
- a health and safety review service for publishers, exam boards and other organisations producing teaching resources.

The findings also highlighted specific misconceptions, including that '70% think it is illegal for pupils to sample their own blood and 32% . . . believe pupils cannot experiment on their own saliva samples' (Royal Society of Chemistry 2007).

Table 7.1 explains why the above beliefs are misconceptions. In addition, 10–30 per cent of respondents to the RSC survey also believed, wrongly, that more than 15 other chemicals and activities were banned.

Actually, very few STEM activities and chemicals which schools might consider using are banned, at least at a national level. In Science, for example, the major ones banned include:

- benzene and solutions containing benzene
- various ozone depleters
- some radioactive sources
- making explosives, including dissecting fireworks, though firing ready-made rockets is fine with suitable precautions (Table 7.1)
- anything involving cruelty to vertebrates
- anything involving removal of protected species from the wild.

School governing bodies, advisors and inspectors employed by local authorities can also direct teachers not to use particular chemicals or activities; if you believe this to be a misconception on their part, do argue for your students to have the best experiences if you feel confident to do so.

Some teachers may not have had experience, when they were students themselves, or during teacher training, of the more dramatic practicals. Attending courses run by CLEAPSS, Science Learning Centres or other appropriate organisations could help to provide personal confidence to conduct suitably informed risk assessments and argue against any mistakenly imposed banned protocols.

On a positive note, the RSC survey did find that exciting activities were still being undertaken, such as:

- 97 per cent of schools demonstrate the reaction between potassium and water
- 96 per cent demonstrate the van der Graaf generator
- 90 per cent dissect a heart.

School visits and trips

Well-managed school trips and outdoor activities are great for children. Children won't learn about risk if they're wrapped in cotton wool.

(Health and Safety Executive 2011a)

Whether visiting local hedgerows, design museums, university computer science departments, theme parks for a Physics day out or expeditions abroad, there are innumerable benefits in getting out and doing things beyond the classroom.

The Council for Learning Outside the Classroom is the national 'voice' for learning outside the classroom. They believe that every young person, 0–19 years, should experience the world beyond the classroom as an essential part of learning and personal development. Their website has a range of resources to support working with students beyond the classroom, including visits and trips.

Misunderstandings about the application of health and safety law may discourage some schools and teachers from organising trips. Government advice about planning for activities happening out of the school grounds includes:

If these are annual or infrequent activities, a review of an existing assessment may be all that is needed. For any new visit or activity, a specific assessment of risks must be carried out. Headteachers should ensure that the person assigned with the assessment task understands the risks and is familiar with the activity that is planned.

(Department for Education 2012b)

The head teacher should keep a record of all risk assessments associated with visits.

Some schools and teachers have concerns about being prosecuted if an accident occurs during a trip away from school. The policy statement 'School trips and outdoor learning activities: Tackling the health and safety myths' (Health and Safety Executive 2011a) explains that the real issues are risks arising from serious breaches of the law, such as students going out on a boat but the trip leader not ensuring that all wore life jackets (Figure 7.1).

Legal action for negligence against schools is only likely to be successful if:

- the school has not taken care of a child in a way that a prudent parent would have done
- as a result, the child has been injured and
- the injury was a foreseeable consequence (Department for Education 2012b).

Trips abroad

Schools must consider their duties under health and safety law when planning trips abroad. The Health and Safety Executive has a 'frequently asked questions' web page on school trips that provides useful guidance.

Most trips abroad with well-established companies are likely to come with ready-made risk assessments. These still have to be checked and amended as appropriate; for example, getting to an airport may not be included in the company's risk assessment.

Figure 7.1 One of the authors and Year 11–13 students on an expedition to the Peruvian Amazon to study biodiversity.

Note: Everyone is wearing a buoyancy aid. Not sure how these aids would have protected against the piranhas, though.

One of the authors has been fortunate in being able to take students abroad on expeditions to Malaysia, working in an elephant sanctuary and to Peru, working on Amazonian biodiversity. Advance planning and enjoyable research allowed the Department for Education (2012b) requirement of 'understands the risks and is familiar with the activity that is planned' to be met. The efforts in writing risk assessments and other paperwork were more than compensated for by the tremendous impact on the students, and author, of these visits.

Driving the school minibus

School staff may drive a school minibus without a special licence, as long as their employer agrees and as long as the following conditions are met:

- their car driving licence was obtained before January 1997 or
- their car driving licence was obtained after January 1997 and has been held for at least 2 years and no payment for driving is involved and the minibus weighs no more than 3.5 tonnes and is not being used for hire or reward (Department for Education 2012b).

There may be local requirements that go beyond the basic conditions set out by the Department for Education. These are likely to include the need for an additional driver to be present and limits to lengths of driving times without a break.

Common sense suggests, and probably most schools will as well, that any first-time drivers go out with a more experienced driver for a practice drive before taking pupils as passengers. There are likely to be various safety checks that the school requires to be completed and the school may offer or insist on further training.

Parental consent to off-site activities

During usual school hours, written consent from parents is not required for students, older than nursery age, to take part in most off-site activities organised by a school. This is because such activities are considered to be a normal part of a school education.

However, parents should be told where their child is going and of any extra safety measures required (Department for Education 2013a). Most schools will have this written into their 'home-school' agreement.

Officially (following the Department for Education), parental written consent is usually only required for activities:

- needing a higher level of risk management
- happening outside school hours.

As most trips and visits involve travelling, and so increased risk, the school may feel parental consent is necessary.

The Department for Education (2013a) has produced a 'one-off' consent form that parents can sign when their child starts at a school. This should cover participation in activities throughout their time at the school, including visits to museums, exploratories, STEM fairs and residential visits. Find out if your school has adopted this form or whether your school has its own system for obtaining parental consent.

Parents must be told in advance about off-site activities and be given the opportunity to withdraw their child from particular school trips or visits.

Risk assessments

There are many sources of advice and templates available for risk assessments. Your school is likely to have existing risk assessments that can be updated or templates to use. In local authority-managed schools, the local authority often determines these.

The Health and Safety Executive (2012a) leaflet, 'Five steps to risk assessment', explains how to create risk assessments for the workplace. Although not school-specific, it is a useful and simple guide, with a risk assessment template on the last page.

The five steps given in this leaflet are:

1   Identify the hazards.
2   Decide who might be harmed and how.
3   Evaluate the risks and decide on precaution.
4   Record your findings and implement them.
5   Review your assessment and update if necessary.

To help identify the hazards and evaluate the risks (Box 7.2) in school and when working outside or going on visits, you need to consider the:

1   age and ability of the students
2   maturity and behaviour of the students
3   level of supervision they will receive
4   extent of technician or other support
5   size and layout of any work area
6   types of activities
7   competence and experience of the teacher
8   likely weather conditions if working outdoors (and if appropriate, tide times, river levels and flow rates)
9   health and safety arrangements of venues.

It is also important to take into account:

10   students with special educational needs or disabilities
11   students with English as an additional language.

Box 7.2   Check those terms

Hazard: anything that might cause harm, e.g. particular chemicals, sharp instruments, moving machinery

Risk: the likelihood or chance, low or high, that somebody could be harmed if exposed to a hazard

Of course, an activity deemed entirely appropriate for a small group of 16-year-old students with an experienced teacher might not be suitable for a class of 11-year-olds with an inexperienced teacher.

When evaluating any risk, you need to take into account how likely it is that someone may be harmed plus the potential severity of the outcome should anyone be harmed. If either the potential risk or severity of outcome is deemed too high to be acceptable, then ways to reduce the risk should be considered. If it cannot be reduced, then an alternative activity has to be found. However, most hazards are either well known or can be anticipated and appropriate precautions implemented.

A particularly useful source of advice and templates for risk assessments is CLEAPSS (Box 7.1). Most UK schools and teacher-training institutes have membership. CLEAPSS has many guidance leaflets about managing risk assessments in Science and Design & Technology. They provide model risk assessments as well as templates for specific activities. Particularly helpful advice, which encourages students to create their own risk assessments, is given in two CLEAPSS publications:

- Making and recording risk assessments in school Science
- Student Safety Sheets which guide pupils through the thinking process of assessing risks.

DATA, the Design and Technology Association (2008), has a useful booklet, *Risk Assessment in Secondary Schools and Colleges*, which provides clear health and safety guidance for D&T teaching environments, as well as blank templates for writing risk assessments, with helpful notes.

Risk assessments cannot cover every eventuality, particularly unexpected accidents. For example, during a Science lesson on food tests a student ended up with a deep cut due to snapping dry pasta to fit into a test tube. Such an injury had not been thought possible when the original risk assessment was written for this practical. The edge of the pasta was sharp enough to inflict a cut that almost required stitches. Following this incident, future practicals used cooked pasta!

Another example of an unexpected accident was during a class visit to a bird sanctuary. The teacher had carried out a pre-visit and produced a risk assessment. However, on arrival a student stepped out of the minibus and immediately put her foot on a rusty nail that pierced both shoe and foot. Fortunately, the risk assessment had identified that the sanctuary had a first-aid post and the teacher had brought copies of the students' medical records with her, but the accident could not have been anticipated.

As long as risk assessments cover likely hazards, there should be no blame attached to the teacher or leader if an accident occurs in or out of school. After the pasta and rusty nail incidents described above, accident reports were filed (see following section on reporting accidents), the students recovered and no fault was found with any of the procedures or staff involved.

Training

Employers must ensure that their staff have appropriate health and safety training for their jobs. As a minimum, this could mean providing staff with health and safety information relevant to the school, perhaps via the school's health and safety policy document. However, most schools are likely to offer further training, perhaps via sessions in school or to support requests to attend training courses where there is a clear link to the responsibilities of a member of staff's job role.

Staff involved in activities with obvious risks such as using woodworking machines will need more training. More information about training is available on the Health and Safety Executive website (Health and Safety Executive 2011a) and from the Department for Education (2012b). Chapter 4 also has suggestions about specific training for STEM club leaders.

Reporting injuries and accidents

Certain work-related injuries must, by law, be recorded and reported. The employer is responsible for this, though staff may prepare the report.

Guidance for schools on what, how, where and when to report is explained in the Health and Safety Executive's leaflet (2012b) 'Incident reporting in schools (accidents, diseases and dangerous occurrences)'.

Make sure that you are familiar with your school's health and safety policy. This should make it clear what you have to do if an injury or accident occurs when you are in charge. Usually it means filling in a template with details about the incident, within a certain time of the incident. The school will keep a copy of this. Such documentation is useful if there are any queries about what happened.

Staff/student ratios

It is useful for organisers to know what staff/student ratios are expected for practical lessons, outdoor activities, trips and school clubs. However, there are no generally agreed or prescribed ratios. The following gives some guidance for activities in and out of school.

Indoor practical work

The British Standards Institution (2007) publishes a *Code of Practice* that gives advice on health and safety in Design & Technology. This recommends, for England and Wales, that 'the recommended maximum number of students in any one work area is 20 students with one competent, qualified teacher'.

This could equally apply to practical work in any STEM subject, though common sense should be used about the maturity and behaviour of groups. There are legal requirements in Scotland and Northern Ireland for all classes in practical subjects to be restricted to a maximum of 20 students.

Outdoor activities, such as practical work in school grounds

An adequate ratio of adults to pupils is needed in order to ensure that the intended activities are performed safely. The precise ratio will be determined by the risk assessment. It should not be assumed that the normal level of pupil supervision that applies in laboratories or classrooms will be appropriate out of doors.

(CLEAPSS 2006a)

The risk assessment should consider what is an appropriate teacher/student ratio for working outside; this will be influenced by the nature of the activity and the age/maturity/behaviour of the pupils. The school or local authority may have regulations about supervision, so it is useful to check what is in place already.

Outdoor activities, such as fieldwork beyond the school grounds

Staff leading field trips should be supported by at least one other adult; most local authorities have rules about the ratio of adults to students for different ages of student and type of trip.

Do check your own school requirements as they may have specific guidance that you need to follow.

Academies, not working with local authorities, are likely to have their own regulations or recommendations. Where there are no local regulations or guidance, it may be useful to note that a ratio of two adults per group of 20 students, with an extra adult for up to 10 additional pupils in larger group sizes, was recommended by CLEAPSS, though this goes back more than 20 years (CLEAPSS 1991).

There are many different activities that may be considered 'fieldwork'. Some of these may require different staff/student ratios. For example, activities involving water may require more staff per student.

School trips

> Pupil to staff ratios for school trips are not prescribed in law. Those planning trips, on the basis of risk assessment, should decide the ratios, taking into account the activity to be undertaken and the age and maturity of the pupils.
>
> (Health and Safety Executive 2012a)

It is advisable always to have adult back-up; for example, if a member of staff or student becomes ill during a trip, then there is someone to take over or to stay with the group while the sick person is looked after. This is normally written into school/local authority regulations about trips and staff/student ratios. Remember that all adults, apart from supervised volunteers, will need to have been checked by the Disclosure and Barring Service (DBS). Further information can be found via the Home Office (2013).

Additionally, it is worth checking whether the venue has specific requirements. Some state that they expect a certain number of staff to accompany students. Some venues may be more stringent than schools.

Taking photographs and films of students

Photos and videos of activities and students enjoying activities make great promotional material for the school and/or STEM club. Of course, they also make wonderful records for the students themselves and for parents to share. However, there is concern about when it is, and when it is not, appropriate to take photographs or other visual records.

The Data Protection Act (see later in this chapter) applies to photos or films taken for official school use, but not to photos or films taken for personal use. When photos are taken for official use such as putting on the school website, in a school prospectus or in a local newspaper, letting guardians and students know the context that the photo will be used in, and obtaining their permission, is usually sufficient to comply with the Act.

Further guidance about taking photos or films of students may be obtained from the Information Commissioner's Office (undated).

Eating and drinking in labs, computer rooms and workrooms

Guidance (CLEAPSS 2006b, c) is that no eating and drinking should take place in areas that could be contaminated with chemicals, hazardous microorganisms or anything liable to contaminate what is ingested. A separate 'clean' area is always the preferred option. Most computer rooms do not allow eating or drinking and such school rules need to be followed, even out of school hours.

Some key advisory bodies

The rest of this chapter give some key sources of further information. Other sources, and further details of the bodies listed, are given in Chapter 9.

- Association for Science Education (ASE)
- British Science Association
- British Standards Institution education website
- CLEAPSS
- Council for Learning Outside the Classroom (CLOtC)
- Design and Technology Association (DATA)
- Engineering Development Trust (EDT)
- Health and Safety Executive
- Institute of Food Science and Technology
- Institute of Physics
- Mathematical Association
- National STEM Centre
- Royal Academy of Engineering
- Royal Society of Chemistry
- Society of Biology
- STEMNET
- Young Engineers.

Some key legislation related to STEM activities

Child protection legislation in the UK

The National Society for the Prevention of Cruelty to Children (NSPCC 2012) has a useful downloadable pdf about this legislation.

COSHH Regulations, 2002

Advice and information about the Control of Substances Hazardous to Health is given on the Health and Safety Executive (2013a) website.

Data Protection Act, 1998

Legal obligations to protect personal information affect keeping registers and taking photographs/making videos. Advice about the Act may be found via the Information Commissioner's Office (2013). A BBC website (2013) helps ICT students understand this Act; these could be useful for an easy overview.

Disclosure and Barring Service, 2012

The Criminal Records Bureau and Independent Safeguarding Authority merged at the end of 2012 to become the Disclosure and Barring Service (DBS). The DBS helps prevent unsuitable people from working with vulnerable groups, including children. Further information can be found via the Home Office (2013).

Health & Safety at Work etc. Act, 1974

This Act is the primary piece of legislation for occupational health and safety in Great Britain. Basic information about this Act is given on the Health and Safety Executive webpage: 'Health and Safety Made Simple'.

Management of Health and Safety at Work Regulations, 1999

Dealing with basic health and safety arrangements, and risk assessments, these regulations also have information about expectant mothers and 'young persons' as well as training requirements. The Health and Safety Executive webpage: 'Management of Health and Safety at Work' has further information.

Manufacture and Storage of Explosives Regulations, 2005

These regulations are relevant for anyone considering making or using rockets (powered by explosives), fireworks or gunpowder. CLEAPSS (2008) has guidance on the use of fireworks and explosives in schools that addresses the 2005 regulations and lists what may and may not be done in school.

Provision and Use of Work Equipment Regulations, 1998

A simple guide to these regulations can be downloaded from the Health and Safety Executive website (Health and Safety Executive 2008). They are particularly useful for certain equipment, such as woodworking machines and power presses that may be used in Design & Technology and Engineering.

REACH Regulation, 2007

REACH is a European Union regulation concerning the Registration, Evaluation, Authorisation and restriction of Chemicals. CLEAPSS has a free guidance leaflet about how the REACH regulation applies to the use of chemicals in school Chemistry activities (CLEAPPS 2011).

Waste Electrical and Electronic Equipment Regulations, 2006

Also known as the WEEE Regulations, these aim to reduce the amount of waste electrical or electronic equipment being disposed of in landfill by encouraging separate collection, treatment and recycling. These regulations may be of particular interest to Eco clubs or clubs interested in sustainability. Further information can be found via the UK Environmental Law Association (2011).

All these regulations and legislation help ensure the safety of you and your students. They are given here to be of use should you wish to check anything, but our message is that you can do it and be safe.

Additional guidance: books and documents

- Departmental Advice on Health and Safety for Schools (Department for Education 2012b)
- Frequently Asked Questions – Education / School Trips etc. (Health and Safety Executive undated)
- Guidance to Inspecting e-safety (Ofsted 2012a)
- Health and Safety, Frequently Asked Questions (DATA 2013)
- Licence to Cook Case Studies – Health and Safety (Department for Education 2000–2009)
- Notes for STEM clubs and STEM ambassador resources, a list of some common potential hazards and suggested control measures (Royal Academy of Engineering 2011)
- Oh Yes You Can; Safety Matters (Association for Science Education 2007)
- Safe and Exciting Science (Association for Science Education 2010)
- Safeguarding Changes – January 2013 (Success in Schools 2013)
- Safeguards in the School Lab (Association for Science Education 2006)
- Safety in Practical Lessons (http://www.teachers.org.uk/node/12547)
- Surely that's banned? (Royal Society of Chemistry 2007)
- The Bristol Guide (University of Bristol Graduate School of Education 2012, updated yearly)

Chapter 8

Obtaining and making the most of funding

By the end of this chapter, you will have ideas about how to:

- make the most of available funds
- obtain further funding
- generate income.

Successfully incorporating engaging and enhancing STEM activities into lessons and beyond lessons, e.g. visits or as part of a STEM club, is likely to require additional funding.

This chapter explores some options related to funding.

Making the most of any available funds

Find out what budgets are available to you and whether any are available for extension work. You may have to make a case, perhaps to the Senior Leadership Team or to a Parents' Association, for additional funding for new projects or for starting up a STEM club. Chapter 2 has ideas to help make a strong case.

Once you have found out what your budget is, then you can start to be creative with it. Figure 8.1 suggests some ideas to extend a budget.

Making a little go a long way requires planning and careful choice of materials. One example comes from plant Biology. Figure 8.2 shows the many uses of a cheap and easily available plant, the African violet, *Saintpaulia* sp.

There are many items, other than plants, with the potential to be used in many ways. For example, our trainee teachers came up with 50 inexpensive STEM-related ideas using balloons.

Making use of scrap and recycled materials can provide a variety of kit to work with, though health and safety issues will need considering, as might storage issues. Such materials may be obtained from:

- Resource exchanges. Most cities have these, or similar. They are ideal for finding offcuts and excess materials, usually donated by local industries. We have seen such scrap items used to make buggies, 'whoosh' rockets and bottle gardens.
- Freecycle. These online groups match people who have things they don't want with people who can use them, with the aim of keeping items out of landfills. Registration with your local group is free and then you just have to check for updates. This is ideal for items like fish tanks for vivariums and used Chemistry sets.
- Friendly retailers. Bike shops are useful for old tyre tubing, which makes good connectors for 'whoosh' rockets; photography outlets usually have supplies of film canisters that can be used for baking powder and vinegar 'explosions'.

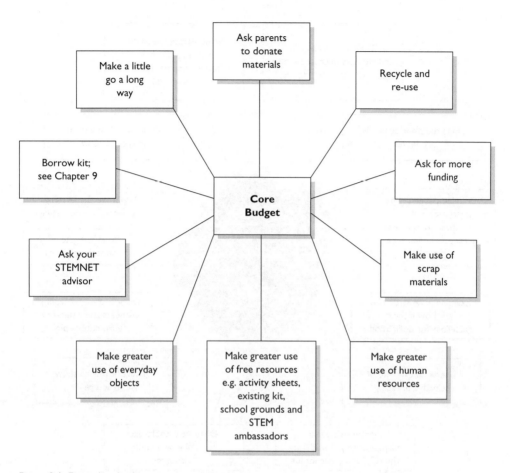

Figure 8.1 Extending budgets.

One resource not to be overlooked is that supplied by people. Table 5.2 in Chapter 5 lists people who can provide help, but the students themselves can, within ethical guidelines, act as subjects for investigations. These may range from measuring finger length for statistical surveys through to more exotic investigations such as whether telepathy exists.

Another way of running activities on a small budget is to borrow or share equipment. Use of the school grounds and local environment also costs nothing, though you may need to ask permission of any local landowners for access.

A vast array of resources, many of them free of charge or low-cost, has been developed by a range of providers to support STEM activities. Chapter 9 has further information about some of these.

Obtaining further funding

However creative your use of existing resources, sometimes there will be a need for more financial input. Funding can range from small grants to major input, such as North East

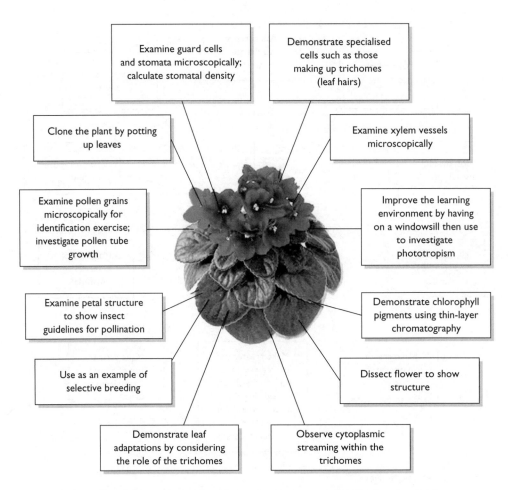

Figure 8.2 Extending resources, using the African violet as an example. Further details about some of the protocols can be found on the Science and Plants for Schools website.

Wolverhampton Academy's 2-year project with Boeing to build and fly a microlight plane at a cost of £40,000 (Paczuska and Steedman 2012).

Table 8.1 suggests ways of obtaining funding. Undoubtedly, some examples given here will change and new ones appear, so treat the examples as generic ones and keep a look out for new sources and opportunities. Table 8.2 recommends some fundraising guides.

Although many organisations provide grants, there are other people competing for these. You are more likely to succeed if you can show the wider impact of your project and how what you do will benefit others beyond your specific group. Figure 8.3 suggests other ways to increase your chance of success.

Examples in the Association for Science and Discovery Centres/STEMNET guide and our own knowledge show that STEM clubs do attract grants. We hope that you now have greater confidence to apply for one or more of these.

Table 8.1 Sources of funding

Potential source of funding	Examples and/or comments
Your school or department	Find out about current priorities and improvement plans. These might include working with 'feeder' schools or before/after-school provision. If you can contribute towards these, you are more likely to get funding
	Offer to save the school money, e.g. through a project that might reduce the school's energy use, for a proportion of the savings in return
	Approach your Parent Teacher Association or equivalent. This is most likely to be successful if linked to a specific project or piece of equipment
Local business and organisations with STEM links	You may receive some financial support in return for advertising, e.g. in the school's newsletter or an article in the local newspaper
	Be prepared to accept non-financial offers of staff time, workshop space, materials or equipment loans
Professional bodies, associations and organisations	See advice in Figure 8.3 about successful grant applications:
	1 The Royal Society of Chemistry has a small grants scheme for activities involving the wider community
	2 The Institute of Physics Public Engagement Grant Scheme is aimed at making Physics more accessible for more people
	3 The Royal Institution grants are designed to encourage enrichment and enhancement activities in Mathematics across a wide age range of students
	4 The National Centre for Excellence in the Teaching of Mathematics provides funding for teachers to work collaboratively
	5 The Royal Society Partnership grants provide funding for schools to run innovative projects in partnership with professional scientists or engineers
	6 Royal Academy of Engineering provides start-up grants for engineering clubs
	7 The British Ecological Society offers outreach grants to support projects that inspire people of all ages about ecology
	8 The British Society for the History of Science offers grants for innovative teaching of, and projects about, the history of Science, Technology and Medicine
	9 The Biochemical Society offers outreach grants for teachers of all age students, particularly in the biosciences fields
	10 The British Science Association coordinates a 'kick start' grant for National Science and Engineering Week, specially for schools in challenging circumstances

(continued)

Table 8.1 (continued)

Potential source of funding	Examples and/or comments

Research and other councils	1 The Science and Technology Facilities Council and the Institute of Physics have a small grants scheme for all UK schools and colleges catering for students aged 5–18. This provides up to £500 for projects or events linked to the teaching or promotion of Physics. Projects linked to astronomy, space and particle physics are particularly encouraged. Grants can be used to:
	
	   • run a science week activity
	   • purchase materials/resources outside normal department resources
	   • organise a visit to or from a working physicist
	
	2 The Arts Council for England provides grants to promote the arts. Architecture and Design can fall under this remit. For example, a primary school was awarded a grant of £2000 to fund a 'Spaghetti Architecture' day learning about design, structure and materials.
	
	3 The Engineering and Physical Sciences Research Council administer the Holmes Hines memorial fund. This provides awards in Science and Engineering e.g.:
	
	   • support for Summer Science Camp
	   • contributions towards the running of Schools' Science Weeks
	   • support for Science and Engineering Clubs
	   • support for Formula1 and Green Power Car Kit projects

The STEM Directories	The STEM Directories (Chapter 9) offer grants of up to £500 for STEM enrichment and enhancement activities in school.
Specific funds and trusts	The Armourers & Brasiers Gauntlet Trust supports Materials Science, the discipline most aligned with the Company's ancient trade of metalworking. Schools can receive grants for projects and equipment that nurture achievement and enthusiasm among primary and secondary school students. The Edina Trust provides non-competitive, easy-to-access grants, for state primary schools in certain regions of the UK to promote Science and gardening.
Lottery Awards	Some networks have received grants from 'National Lottery Awards for All' e.g. the Maths and Art Club network in York. 'Awards for All' is a Lottery grants scheme funding small, local community-based projects.
European Union Awards	EU funding such as Comenius may be available for projects involving partner schools abroad. In EiSXtra (2013), Hughes describes some exciting STEM club events made possible by various grants and offers to give advice to others interested in applying for EU grants.
Charity Directories/ Funding databases	To find details of local education grants or subject support it is probably best to 'Google' what you are looking for or use your local library.

Table 8.2 Further guides for fundraising

STEMNET	The UK Association for Science and Discovery Centres in association with STEMNET has produced a *Fundraising Guide for STEM Clubs*. This useful guide includes: • a database of funders • practical advice on writing to funding bodies and businesses • examples of matched funding • examples of projects that have received funding (http://sciencecentres.org.uk/resources/stemclubs/)
Fundraising for schools	*Fundraising for Schools* is a monthly magazine offering information about financial grants and awards for schools. It includes best practice on applying for grants and advice and ideas for school fundraising (www.fundraisingschools.co.uk)
Specific guides	For environmental work across all age ranges CLEAPSS (1998) produced a booklet, L221 *Developing and Using Environmental Areas in School Grounds,* which has a useful section on fundraising. Despite being produced in 1998, this suggests useful strategies and guides you through approaching sponsors and applying for grants 'Finding funding for Science and Engineering projects': useful article in *Primary Science* by the Education Outreach Manager at the Royal Society (Helm 2012)

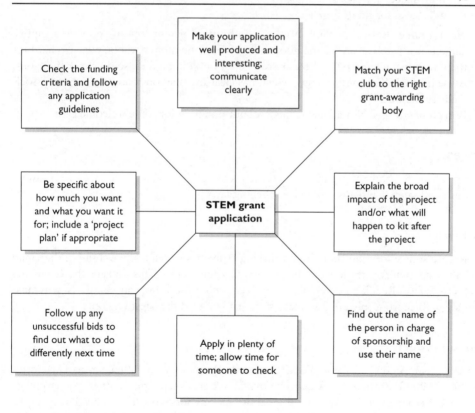

Figure 8.3 Successful grant applications.

Generating income

This final section looks at how to generate income. This can be the quickest way to bring in funds. Sometimes you may be offered a 'matching' grant, when money is offered to match whatever is raised. Students are more likely to appreciate money that they have earned.

Suggestions for raising money:

1 Make a product and sell it. This can involve production, packaging and advertising. A STEM club from a school in Devon took their scented lip balms to the Big Bang Fair in 2012, sold everything and made £160 profit (Howarth and Scott 2012). Another successful project by a different school was to sell not just 'bath bombs' but kits to make bath bombs. They also sold all their products.

2 Grow a product and sell it. Garden mint grows in most soils, so it is easy to cultivate in school grounds. A few years ago, a competition called Making a Mint sent schools, on request, packets of mint seeds and encouraged students to be commercially innovative with their plants. The competition is now finished, but for little more than the price of a packet of seeds, students could still produce a variety of products to sell, such as:

- dried mint
- potted mint plants
- mint sauce
- a '50 uses for mint' booklet.

3 Hold a raffle. Both for selling products and raffles, parents' events provide a captive audience. If parents can see the good use to which the money will be put, it is hard for them to resist helping out. There are rules about holding raffles, so do check these out. A useful site is 'RaisingFunding', which has clear explanations about raffles and associated regulations.

4 Win competitions. Not a reliable income, but potential for some welcome cash.

Notes

With products for human use, whether cosmetics or edible products, you need to be aware of health and safety legislation as well as labelling laws.

Cosmetics

A reference source for regulations about making cosmetics to sell is the website of the Guild of Craft Soap and Toiletry Makers (http://www.gcstm.co.uk). This explains the Cosmetics Products (Safety) Regulations, legislation in force within the European Union. New regulations are in force from July 2013 so make sure that you read the latest version.

Edible products

The National Archives of the Food Standards Agency (http://tna.europarchive.org/ 20100929190231/http://www.eatwell.gov.uk/asksam/keepingfoodsafe/asksamevents/) have answers to frequently asked questions about making food to sell at events. For example, the Food Labelling Regulations, 1996, apparently don't apply to food that isn't prepared as part of a business. However, food that is attractively and informatively labelled is more likely to sell well. The archives also have common-sense recommendations about food hygiene and the transport and storage of food.

Chapter 9

Resources

Where to find resources and how to make the most of them

By the end of this chapter, you will know where to find relevant resources from:

- organisations and websites
- books and ebooks
- Twitter.

There are many valuable resources available for use within STEM lessons and clubs. Human resources such as school staff, students, parents and STEM ambassadors have been considered in previous chapters and are probably amongst the greatest resources you can have. This chapter focuses on other available resources, shown in Figure 9.1, many of which are free or low-cost.

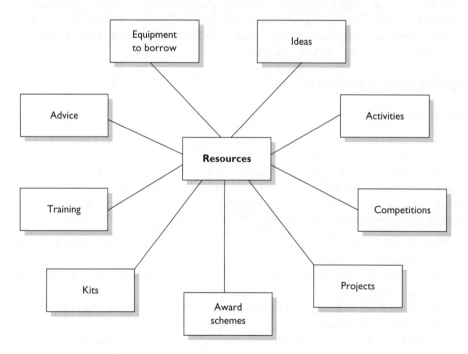

Figure 9.1 Resources for STEM lessons and clubs.

Borrowing kit

A number of organisations loan materials. These include:

- Local and regional branches of some professional bodies and organisations and local delivery teams for national projects. The availability of resources that can be borrowed can vary a lot. Use your local STEMNET contract holder to find out what is currently available in your area.
- National organisations. Examples include:
  - o Junior Engineers for Britain loan K'nex kits for use with all age ranges to work on sustainable engineering projects. Case Study 5.3 in Chapter 5 has further details.
  - o The Science and Technology Facilities Council loans moon rocks.

  STEMNET contract holders can also advise on new national ventures.

Resource lists

The rest of this chapter lists resources organised as 'general STEM' and as separate subjects. There is quite a lot of overlap, so it is worth searching beyond specific categories.

Undoubtedly, some weblinks will alter with time. Care has been taken to select substantial organisations, likely to be around for a long time, so if a weblink fails to work, returning to the organisation's home page and searching using key words should find most missing pages and probably bring up new ones.

Note that some resources, especially those that suggest activities that can be done at home, may not provide risk assessments or, if they do, they may not be adequate. Chapter 7 has advice on risk assessments.

Finally, if the following lists do not provide sufficient, suitable resources, then our recommendation is to visit The Big Bang Fair (or a regional version). No one can visit one of these without coming away inspired and full of ideas for things to do, including how to access new resources for activities to use back at school.

Organisations and websites

General STEM

All Science Fair Projects – an encyclopedia: http://www.all-science-fair-projects.com/science_fair_projects_encyclopedia.

Association for Science and Discovery Centres/STEMNET guide: links to resources that help with fundraising: http://sciencecentres.org.uk/resources/stemclubs.

BBC, Great Egg Race (archive): http://www.bbc.co.uk/archive/great_egg_race.

British Science Association:

- Case Studies and Ideas for Projects: http://www.britishscienceassociation.org/crest-awards/case-studies.
- CREST Awards covering all STEM subjects: http://www.britishscienceassociation.org/crest-awards.
- CREST 'Pick Up & Run' project resources section has 27 ideas to help you get started: http://www.britishscienceassociation.org/crestresources.
- CREST in a day: http://apstemactivities.weebly.com/crest-in-a-day.html.
- CREST Ideas for Bronze, Silver and Gold projects: http://www.britishscienceassociation.org/crest-awards/project-ideas.
- CREST Star Sample Activities: http://www.britishscienceassociation.org/crest-star-sample-activities.

- Download Hub has resources, guides about CREST, other schemes and useful forms: http://www.britishscienceassociation.org/crest-awards/download-hub.
- National Science and Engineering Week pages: www.britishscienceassociation.org/national-science-engineering-week.
- STEM Club Leader training: http://www.britishscienceassociation.org/crest-awards/clubs-support/club-leader-events-things-think-about.

The British Society for the History of Science (BSHS): histories of science, technology and medicine and their changing relationship with society; some useful information for projects: http://www.bshs.org.uk.

The British Society for the History of Science Travel Guide to Scientific Sites: information about places around the world that link to the history of Science, Technology and Medicine: http://www.bshs.org.uk/travel-guide.

British Standards Institution Education website: activities about alternative energy, applied science, bicycles, bridges, through to sustainability and toys: http://www.bsieducation.org/Education/14-19/default.shtml.

CLEAPSS: advisory service for Science and Design & Technology: Box 7.1 in Chapter 7 has more information: http://www.cleapss.org.uk.

CLOtC, Council for Learning Outside the Classroom: the national organisation for learning outside the classroom: http://www.lotc.org.uk.

Computing At School: the subject association for computer science: http://community.computingatschool.org.uk.

Decipher My Data, via I'm a Scientist: Maths and Science project for 11–16-year-olds using real school data: http://flu.deciphermydata.org.uk.

Eco-Schools England: an international award programme that guides schools towards becoming sustainable: http://www2.keepbritaintidy.org/ecoschools/abouteco schools.

EducaPoles, the educational website of the International Polar Foundation: http://www.educapoles.org.

Equality and Diversity Toolkit for STEM: downloadable pdf, free registration required: http://digitalstorecupboard.tintisha-web.co.uk/equality-and-diversity.

For Girls in Science: addresses all STEM subjects: http://forgirlsinscience.org.

Future Morph: the Science Council-led STEM careers website aimed at young people: http://www.futuremorph.org/teachers/teaching-resources/future-morph-presentation.

GEMS CLUB: creating and managing a STEM club for girls (USA): http://gemsclub.org/starting_a_club.

GetSET Women: speaker and role model database: http://www.wisecampaign.org.uk/get-involved/networks/getset-women.

Go4SET: 10-week STEM team challenge, for 12–13-year-olds, linking schools, companies and universities. See also the Engineering Development Trust: http://www.etrust.org.uk/go4set.cf.

Gocracker: industry-sponsored gateway to hundreds of websites for young engineers and scientists with career, apprenticeship and training advice, resources, apps and a monthly competition: www.Gocracker.com.

Good Practice: STEM Subject Choice and Careers, downloadable document for practical hints on how to make materials more inclusive: http://www.stem-e-and-d-toolkit.co.uk.

How to Smile: Science and Maths activities to help those who teach students in non-classroom settings from the New York Hall of Science and other trusted sources: http://www.howtosmile.org.

InGenious: the platform of the European Coordinating Body in STEM education, aiming to reinforce young Europeans' interest in STEM education and careers: http://www.ingenious-science.eu/web/guest/home.

Inspiring the Future: scheme to help professionals come into schools to talk about careers, at no cost to the school. Speakers are currently not checked by the Disclosure and Barring Service, so make sure that your school is fine with this before using this scheme: http://www.inspiringthefuture.org.

Kids school: eco learning European project with Panasonic: http://www.panasonic.co.uk/html/en_GB/About+Panasonic/CSR/CSR%3A+Society/Cross-national+Projects/Kids+school+-+Eco+learning/6627735/index.html.

National Center for Health Statistics: a useful source of data from the US: http://www.cdc.gov/nchs.

National Science and Engineering competition: success stories of winners from 2008 onwards: http://www.nsecuk.org/Success_Stories.

National STEM Centre: UK's largest collection of STEM teaching and learning resources: http://www.nationalstemcentre.org.uk/what-we-offer/overview.

Nuffield Research Placements (previously Nuffield Science bursaries); Box 5.2 in Chapter 5 has information: http://www.nuffieldfoundation.org/nuffield-research-placements.

Open Industry: the Industrial Trust Division of the Engineering Development Trust provides students, 11–18 years, with visits to organisations focused on STEM subjects: http://www.etrust.org.uk/open_industry/about_open_industry.cfm.

Postcards for the Future: downloadable graphic novel showing women and STEM careers: http://www.wisecampaign.org.uk/women/postcards-from-the-future.

Practical Action offers some global issues for students to investigate, such as transporting tomatoes without them becoming squashed and challenges about water, food, shelter, transport and energy, suitable for CREST Awards: http://practicalaction.org.

Primary Engineer: using Maths and Science in Design and Make activities. Also STEM Leaders Awards, open to students aged 5–19 years: http://primaryengineer.com.

RaisingFunding: guidance on running raffles, lotteries and lucky dips: http://www.raisingfunding.co.uk/raffles-lotteries-lucky-dips.html.

Royal Academy of Engineering: teaching and learning resource for 11–14-year-olds that combines STEM activities to investigate big questions: http://www.raeng.org.uk/education/eenp/engineering_resources/Teaching_and_Learning_Resources.htm.

The Royal Society: partnership scheme provides grants: http://royalsociety.org/summer-science.

Science Daily news website: some of the latest Maths and Science research news written in a readable manner: http://www.sciencedaily.com/news/computers_math/mathematics.

Sciencelive: online directory of speakers and presenters for Science and Engineering; see Box 2.1 in Chapter 2: http://www.sciencelive.net.

Scienceshirts, the website for the company producing a tea towel showing British pioneers of Science, Technology and Maths linked to UK locations: http://www.scienceshirts.co.uk.

Skype in the Classroom: Science, Technology and Maths lessons around the world, e.g. Humans in Space, Collaborative Math and Sustainable Farming: https://education.skype.com.

Speakers for Schools database; see Box 2.1 in Chapter 2: http://www.speakers4schools.org.

STEM Central Education in Scotland: http://www.educationscotland.gov.uk/stemcentral/index.asp.

STEM Challenges, 11–14 years: ten activities inspired by the London 2012 Olympics. Archived, but resources still downloadable. A relaunch is expected late 2013: http://www.stemclubs.net/article/241.

STEM Clubs Network (UK): free to join network of STEM clubs managed by STEMNET. Access to project ideas, resources, tips on how to get your club up and running, club leader continuing professional development, events and news about other clubs: http://www.stemclubs.net.

STEM Directories: free online resource for teachers, including speaker searches and grants: http://www.stemdirectories.org.uk.

STEM Diversity and Equality Toolkit: interactive toolkit to help promote STEM careers to 11–16-year-olds from a range of backgrounds and needs: http://www.stem-e-and-d-toolkit.co.uk.

STEMNET: lead organisation in enabling all young people to achieve their potential in STEM; organises the free STEM ambassadors programme with over 27,000 registered volunteers across the UK: http://www.stemnet.org.uk.

STEMWORKS (USA): supports volunteers working in local communities to increase STEM skills: http://www.stem-works.com/about.

Teaching Kids News: relevant news articles for students and educators: http://teachingkids news.com.

TED Talks: non-profit organisation devoted to 'Ideas Worth Spreading'. Started as a conference bringing together people from: Technology, Entertainment and Design, but now a broader scope: http://www.ted.com/pages/about.

The Big Bang Fair: the largest STEM celebration for 7–19-year-old students in the UK, showing the many exciting and rewarding opportunities possible with the right experience and qualifications: http://www.thebigbangfair.co.uk/about_us.cfm.

The Big Bang Near Me: as above, but more local: http://www.thebigbangfair.co.uk/nearme.

The Year in Industry: help with finding work in industry and/or sponsorship post-school: http://www.etrust.org.uk/the_year_in_industry/apply_now.cfm.

UKASD: the UK Association for Science and Discovery Centres – group of 60+ science/STEM engagement organisations in the UK: http://sciencecentres.org.uk/about.

Vital: innovative professional development programme and resources to help Computer Science, Science and Maths teachers bring innovation into the classroom and inspire learners: http://www.vital.ac.uk/ (moving after April 2013 to JISC Advance).

Wellcome Collection: connections between medicine, life and art. Monthly newsletters: http://www.wellcomecollection.org/visit-us/sign-up.aspx.

WISE, Women into Science and Engineering: mission to increase the involvement of women and other underrepresented groups in STEM: http://www.wisecampaign.org.uk/education.

Young Archaeologists Club: activities provide historical contexts for investigative skills linked to health, diet, Design, Technology and Engineering: http://www.nationalstemcentre.org.uk/elibrary/collection/603/young-archaeologists-club.

Young Engineers and Science Clubs (Scotland): aims to engage students in exciting,hands-on Science, Technology and Engineering in school and for careers: http://www.yecscotland.co.uk.

Science

Arizona Science Center: STEM ideas for curriculum and clubs. http://www.azscience.org/who_are_you/stem.

Association for Science Education: promotes excellence in Science teaching and learning; produces guidance on safety issues: http://www.ase.org.uk/home.

AstraZeneca: Introducing Science Clubs and Their Benefits, mainly for under-11s: http://www.azteachscience.co.uk/ext/cpd/science-clubs/index.html.

BBSRC:

- Resources for schools, including ideas for Nuffield Research Placements, Biology in the Real World: http://www.bbsrc.ac.uk/society/schools/schools-index.aspx.
- Vision of the Future Pack, including eye dissections: http://www.bbsrc.ac.uk/web/FILES/Resources/vision-of-the-future.pdf.

Biochemical Society: School Resources: http://www.biochemistry.org/Education/Abouteducation.aspx.

Biology4All: Speakers Database; see Box 2.1 in Chapter 2: http://www.biology4all.com/speakers_database/index.asp.

Biology Challenge: for 13–14-year-olds: http://www.biology-olympiad.org.uk/biology-challenge.

British Biology Olympiad: for 17–19-year-olds: http://www.biology-olympiad.org.uk.

British Physics Olympiad: for 18-year-olds: http://www.physics.ox.ac.uk/olympiad/PaperCompetitions.html.

British Science Association: 300+ activities, useful for National Science and Engineering Week, including Science Busking Pack for all ages: http://www.britishscienceassociation.org/national-science-engineering-week/download-activities-competitions-and-quizzes/activity-packs.

British Science Festival: see Chapter 3. http://www.britishscienceassociation.org/british-science-festival.

Cambridge Chemistry Challenge: web-based monthly competition, open to anyone, any age, from anywhere in the world: http://www.c3l6.org.

Chemistry Olympiad: organised by the Royal Society of Chemistry: http://www.rsc.org/Education/events-and-competitions/Olympiad.

Forensic Outreach: aims to introduce forensic science into Science education but at a cost: http://forensicoutreach.com/january-29th-weekly-forensic-round-up.

Getting Practical: website of the completed 'Improving Practical Work in Science' Project: http://www.gettingpractical.org.uk.

Google Science Fair: see Chapter 3: https://www.googlesciencefair.com/en/2013.

Headstart: trust providing hands-on STEM activities and engineering taster courses to encourage 17-year-old students into technology-based careers: http://www.etrust.org.uk/headstart/what_is_headstart.cfm.

I'm a Scientist, Get Me Out of Here: free online events where school students get to meet and interact with scientists: http://imascientist.org.uk.

In2scienceUK: a non-profit organisation which provides placements for gifted A-level students from low income backgrounds: http://in2scienceuk.org.

i,scientist: programme for students to work in labs in the Science Museum, London: http://www.lottolab.org/articles/iscientist.asp.

Institute of Physics: resources for students and teachers; support from regional coordinators; Physics activity pack for STEM clubs: http://www.iop.org/education/teacher/extra_resources/stem/page_41714.html.

National Science Teachers Association (USA): http://www.nsta.org.

National STEM Centre website: UK's largest collection of STEM teaching and learning resources: http://www.nationalstemcentre.org.uk/what-we-offer/overview.

OPAL surveys: include soil and earthworm; air; water and biodiversity, projects with potential for CREST Awards: http://www.opalexplorenature.org/CRESTsecondary.

Physics Challenge: for 16-year-olds: http://www.physics.ox.ac.uk/olympiad/PaperPhysicsChallenge.html.

Planet Science: Science and Technology resources for under- and over-11s, plus ideas for teachers and parents: http://www.planet-science.com.

Royal Horticultural Society: organises Campaign for School Gardening; supplies free start-up kits to schools: http://www.rhs.org.uk/Children/For-schools.

Royal Society of Chemistry: resources for students and teachers; support from regional coordinators; funding and awards, including Top of the Bench, a national competition for 14–16-year-old students: http://www.rsc.org/Education/events-and-competitions/top-of-the-bench/index.asp.

Salters' Chemistry Camps: 3 days in university across the UK and Ireland for 15-year-olds: http://saltersinstitute.co.uk/camps/camp-news.

Salters' Chemistry Club: chemistry festivals, e-newsletters, posters to advertise your Chemistry club: http://saltersinstitute.co.uk/club/club-news.

Salters' Festivals of Chemistry: see Table 3.8 in Chapter 3: http://saltersinstitute.co.uk/festivals/about-festivals.

Science and Plants for Schools: resources for students of all ages, teachers, technicians and teaching assistants, including newsletters, grants: http://www.saps.org.uk.

Science Year CDs: produced by the Association for Science Eduation for Science Year in 2001, these resources include interactive animations, quizzes, games, cross-curricular activities and ideas for assemblies and careers. Some activities are still great; others are becoming a little dated: www.nationalstemcentre.org.uk/elibrary/collection/133/sycd-science-year.

Scientists in Sport: project activity packs, supported by GSK, tailored to fit CREST: http://www.scientistsinsport.com.

Society of Biology, Bionet: membership scheme for students interested in Biology: http://www.societyofbiology.org/membership/bionet.

Society of Biology, Education: careers and competitions: http://www.societyofbiology.org/education.

The North West Design and Technology Festival: see Table 3.8 in Chapter 3: http://www.edgehill.ac.uk/events/2012/03/24/the-north-west-design-and-technology-festival.

The Royal Institution of Great Britain:

- Christmas lectures: http://www.rigb.org/contentControl?action=displayContent&id=00000001882
- L'Oreal Young Scientist Centre: http://www.rigb.org/contentControl?action=displayContent&id=00000002976
- Maths and Engineering Masterclasses: http://www.rigb.org/contentControl?action=displayContent&id=00000000844.

The Science Museum, London: two activity boxes, to buy, for Science and Engineering Club sessions for students aged 11–14 years to complete bronze CREST Awards.

- Crime Lab challenges students to solve a robbery attempt
- Mars Mission explores the challenges of living on the Red Planet.

http://www.britishscienceassociation.org/crest-awards/project-resources-and-accredited-schemes/accredited-schemes/science-museum-club-boxes.

Stimulating Physics Network: free, 4-day summer schools open to non-specialist teachers of Physics: http://www.stimulatingphysics.org/stimulating-physics-network-schools-summer-schools.htm.

Wellcome Trust: In the Zone, free experiment kits (4–11 and 11–19) sent to all UK schools, linked to the London 2012 Olympic and Paralympic Games: http://www.wellcome.ac.uk/Education-resources/Teaching-and-education/In-the-zone/WTVM051961.htm.

Windows to the Universe: Scientists in Schools section has checklists to help make visits effective; other sections offer resources: http://www.windows2universe.org/teacher_resources/sci_schools/ss_home.html&nl=11.

Technology

4x4 in Schools Team radio control car design challenge: for students 13–18 years old. The challenge involves designing, researching, building and project managing a 4x4 vehicle to enter it into a regional heat: http://www.britishscienceassociation.org/crest-awards/project-resources-and-accredited-schemes/accredited-schemes/4x4-schools.

SCIENCE

TECHNOLOGY

Alu D&T Challenge: free D&T teaching resources for students aged 11–14 years and a challenge to design a sustainable item using aluminium: http://www.aludtchallenge.co.uk.

Cracking Ideas: Wallace and Gromit's World of Invention. Kits to make your own ejector seat, balloon hovercraft, etc.: http://www.bbc.co.uk/bbcone/wallaceandgromit/hands-on.

Design and Technology Association: aims to inspire, develop and support excellence in Design and Technology education for all: https://www.data.org.uk.

- Teaching Tomorrow's Designers and Technologists Today professional development: https://www.sciencelearningcentres.org.uk/audience/secondary-post-16/design-technology/teaching-tomorrow2019s-designers-technologists-today.

Digital Design and Technology Programme: free continuing professional development programme for teachers: http://www.digitaldandt.org/index.php/digital-dat.

F1 in Schools Technology Challenge:

- 11–18-year-old students use software to design, analyse, manufacture, test, and race a miniature compressed air-powered Formula 1 car of the future, racing against other teams in regional, national and international finals: http://www.f1inschools.co.uk.
- A junior version, for 5–11-year-olds, is also available: http://www.f1inschools.co.uk/page--primary-f1-in-schools.html.

FIRST LEGO League: global robotics programme: http://www.britishscienceassociation.org/crest-awards/project-resources-and-accredited-schemes/accredited-schemes/first-lego-league.

Institute of Food Science and Technology: project ideas for students: http://www.ifst.org/education/schools_and_higher_education/teacher_resources.

Institute of Materials, Minerals and Mining (IOM3): Can You Make It? Materials challenges for students aged 8–11 years and information and advice on careers, taster courses and scholarship schemes for a wider range of students: http://www.iom3.org/content/school-and-college-pupils.

Rotary International in Great Britain and Ireland: Technology Tournaments: http://www.ribi.org/what-we-do/youth-competitions-and-awards/ribi-technology-tournament.

Silverstone Design Challenge: students in four age categories: 8–11, 11–14, 14–16 and 16+ focus on Design Technology with a real-world link: http://www.britishscienceassociation.org/crest-awards/project-resources-and-accredited-schemes/accredited-schemes/silverstone-design.

Smallpeice Trust: residential courses at universities and other venues for 14-year-olds cover a wide range of subjects, especially Engineering, Design & Technology: http://www.britishscienceassociation.org/crest-awards/project-resources-and-accredited-schemes/accredited-schemes/smallpeice-trust.

Teachers Underground: Textiles in the Class Room: http://teachersunderground.co.uk/Textiles/Textiles.html.

Technology Student: resources for students and teachers: http://www.technologystudent.com.

The Welding Institute:

- Educational outreach events: www.twiprofessional.com/fab-futures/educational-outreach.
- Welding with chocolate, ages 5–19 years, as seen at The Big Bang Fair: http://www.thebigbangfair.co.uk/viewitem.cfm?cit_id=385203.

Engineering

Bloodhound SSC Schools Engineering Project: for all age students: http://www.blood houndssc.com/education.

Engineering Development Trust: provider of STEM enrichment activities: http://www. etrust.org.uk/go4set.cfm.

- EDT First Edition Days: one-day STEM activities in schools: http://www.etrust.org. uk/First_Edition.cfm.
- Go4SET (see under STEM).

Engineering Education Scheme:

- England and Scotland: teams of 16–17-year-old students and teachers work with local industry on real engineering projects for 6 months: http://www.etrust.org.uk/eese/ about_the_engineering_education_scheme.cfm http://www.etrust.org.uk/eese/what_ is_ees.cfm.
- Wales: designed to encourage 16–18-year-olds to study engineering courses after school. Local companies set real industrial problems for teams to solve, in cooperation with engineers and scientists, over 6 months: http://www.stemcymru.org.uk/ http:// www.stemcymru.org.uk/en/getinvolved/eesw/default.php.

Engineering and Physical Sciences Research Council: case studies and experiments for students: http://www.epsrc.ac.uk/newsevents/casestudies/Pages/casestudies.aspx.

Engineering – Go For It (USA): activities and outreach ideas: http://teachers.egfi-k12.org.

IEEE: 'The World's Largest Professional Organisation for the Advancement of Technology':

- Women into Engineering (2012) 4.5-minute YouTube video featuring women from India: http://www.youtube.com/watch?v=AWYPxDHE0oc.
- Engineering Projects in Community Service: http://www.ieee.org/education_careers/ education/preuniversity/epics_high.html.
- The Teacher In-Service Program: http://www.ieee.org/education_careers/education/ preuniversity/tispt/index.htm.

Imagineering Foundation: introduces 8–16-year-olds to the world of engineering and technology through fun, hands-on activities: http://imagineering.org.uk.

Institution of Civil Engineers: resources for students and teachers: http://www.ice.org.uk/ Education.

Institution of Engineering and Technology: communications innovation challenges, Faraday Challenge Days, electric racing car competitions, debates and more for all age students: http://www.theiet.org/resources/teachers.

Jaguar Land Rover: Inspiring Tomorrow's Engineers: Young Women in the Know programme aims to encourage more young women to consider engineering and manufacturing careers: http://www.automotivecouncil.co.uk/2013/02/jaguar-land-rover-launches-new- education-programme-to-encourage-young-women-to-consider-engineering-careers.

London Engineering Project: useful information on running clubs and making them sustainable: http://www.thelep.org.uk/teachers/engclub http://www.thelep.org.uk/ teachers/engclub/clubsustainability

Royal Academy of Engineering: offers free STEM club leader training, based at your school; engineering box of activities (after training); suite of engineering-based resources for teachers: http://www.raeng.org.uk/education.

Tomorrow's Engineers: links to STEM clubs; help for teachers; pilot roadshow: http://www. tomorrowsengineers.org.uk/get_involved.cfm http://www.bydesign-group.co.uk/news/ tomorrows-engineers.

VEX Robotics Competition: annual competition, successful in the USA, South America and Asia, now taking off in the UK for students aged 11–18 years, but costly: http://www. britishscienceassociation.org/crest-awards/vex-robotics-competition.

Young Engineers: club network with access to resources; ideas for setting up and running clubs; challenges; competitions; case studies of successful clubs for all age students; Knexions scheme for cross-phase clubs: http://www.youngeng.org/home.asp.

Maths

British Computer Society: the Chartered Institute for IT: http://www.bcs.org.

Creativity in Maths: creative problem solving in Mathematics for ages 4–14 years: http:// teachers.guardian.co.uk/teacher-resources/6285/Creativity-in-maths.

IEEE Try Computing: http://www.trycomputing.org.

Jaguar Cars: Maths in Motion Challenge for Schools; Bronze CREST Award scheme for students aged 9–16: http://www.britishscienceassociation.org/crest-awards/project-resources-and-accredited-schemes/accredited-schemes/jaguar-cars-maths-motion.

Make IT Happy: annual competition for students aged 9–11 years, run by the Parliamentary IT Committee: http://makeithappy.cc4g.net.

Math Club: ideas and suggestions, from the American Mathematical Association: http:// amc.maa.org/mathclub/3,0-ideas.shtml.

The Mathematical Association: supports and enhances the teaching and learning of Mathematics and its applications; organises Society of Young Mathematicians for students of all ages: http://www.m-a.org.uk/jsp/index.jsp?lnk=000.

Mathematical Association of America: resources for lessons, clubs and competitions: http:// amc.maa.org/mathclub/6,0-Resources.shtml.

Maths and Art Network: ten ideas for workshops: http://www.mathemagic.org/Maths AndArt/index.htm.

Maths Resources and Blogs: the Guardian newspaper's one-stop shop for 'top resources and blogs with maths news and data': http://www.guardian.co.uk/teacher-network/ teacher-network+education/mathematics?CMP=new_53&j=26291&e=howarthsg@ yahoo.co.uk&l=187_HTML&u=1334296&mid=1059027&jb=1&CMP=.

National Centre for Excellence in Teaching of Mathematics: https://www.ncetm.org.uk.

NRich:

- Enriching Mathematics: http://nrich.maths.org/frontpage.
- Maths materials for STEM clubs: http://nrich.maths.org/8975.

United Kingdom Mathematics Trust: a range of competitions, including the Junior Challenge, Intermediate Challenge, British Mathematical Olympiad: http://www. mathcomp.leeds.ac.uk/individual-competitions/junior-mathematical-olympiad.

Books and e-books

Books appearing in the lists here have been chosen as they either have practical ideas or useful stimulus material for engaging STEM activities, in and out of lessons or provide further theory behind the STEM agenda. Only books published in 2010 or later have been included. The caveat about risk-assessing practicals, at the start of this chapter, applies here as well.

Books are in categories of general STEM and separate STEM subjects, but there will be overlap, so it is worth checking across categories.

General STEM

The National STEM Centre eLibrary has a searchable database with filters by subject, age range, date, publisher, type of material: http://www.nationalstemcentre.org.uk/elibrary.

Advancing the Stem Agenda: Quality Improvement Supports Stem (2012), Cindy P. Veenstra, Fernando F. Padro and Julie A. Furst-Bowe

Animating STEM, an ebook (2013), Vera Saar, http://www.squidoo.com/animating-stem

Big Questions from Little People Answered by Some Very Big People (2012) Gemma Harris (compiler) Over 100 real questions from children answered by scientists and others. Each question could make a topic for a STEM club activity

Connecting Students to Stem Careers: Social Networking Strategies (2011) Camilla Cole

STEM is Elementary: Why Elementary Science, Technology, Engineering, and Mathematics Prepares Students to Beat the Gaps (2012) Glory Oljace and Alexander Everhart

STEM Project-Based Learning: An Integrated Science, Technology, Engineering, and Mathematics (STEM) Approach (2013) Robert Capraro, Mary Capraro and James Morgan

STEM the Tide: Reforming Science, Technology, Engineering, and Math Education in America (2011) David Drew

Teaching Stem in the Early Years: Activities for Integrating Science, Technology, Engineering, and Mathematics (2013) Sally Moomaw

The Case for STEM Education, Grades K-College (2013) Roger Bybee

Science

Backyard Biology: Investigate Habitats Outside Your Door with 25 Projects (Build It Yourself) (2013) Donna Latham and Beth Hetland

Can You Feel the Force? Putting the Fizz Back into Physics (2010 reissue) Richard Hammond. Winner of the Junior Aventis Prize for Science Books in 2007

Cool Chemistry Activities for Girls (2012) Jodi Wheeler-Toppen

Cool Physics Activities for Girls (2012) Suzanne Slade

Cool Science Tricks: 50 Fantastic Feats for Kids of All Ages (2012) Daniel Tatarsky

Do Try This At Home: 28 Spectacular Experiments for Scientists of All Ages (2010, new edition) Jon Milton

Ecology Experiments (Facts on File Science Experiments) (2010) Pamela Walker and Elaine Wood

Exemplary Science for Building Interest in STEM Careers (2012) NSTA Press

Forensics: Uncover the Science & Technology of Crime Scene Investigation (Inquire and Investigate) (2013) Carla Mooney and Samuel Carbaugh

Fun Physics Projects for Tomorrow's Rocket Scientists (2013) Alan Gleue

It's Elementary! Putting the Crackle into Chemistry (2010 reissue) Robert Winston

Naked Eggs & Flying Potatoes: Unforgettable Experiments That Make Science Fun (2011) Steve Spangler

Performing Science: Teaching Chemistry, Physics and Biology Through Drama (2012) Ian Abrahams and Martin Braund (editors)

RHS Ready, Steady, Grow! (2012) Royal Horticultural Society

Save Our Science (2013) Ainissa Ramirez, Kindle single only, TED books

Science Magic: Tricks and Puzzles (2011) Martin Gardner

Slimy Science and Awesome Experiments (2012, new edition) Susan Martineau

The Playground Potting Shed: Gardening with Children Made Simple (2010) Dominic Murphy

The Science and History Project Book: 300 Step-by-Step Fun Science Experiments and History Craft Projects for Home Learning and School Study (2013) Chris Oxlade, Rachel Halstead and Struan Reid

Why Are Orangutans Orange? Science Questions in Pictures with Fascinating Answers (2011) Mick O'Hare (editor)

Why Don't Spiders Stick to Their Webs? And 317 Other Everyday Mysteries of Science (2011 edition) Robert Matthews

Technology

Do Try This At Home: Cook It! 30 Yummy Recipes for Scientists of All Ages (2011) Jon Milton

Food: 25 Amazing Projects: Investigate the History & Science of What We Eat (Build It Yourself) (2010) Kathleen Reilly

Gadgets and Inventions (Young Entrepreneurs Club) (2012) Mike Hobbs

Garbage: Investigate What Happens When You Throw It Out with 25 Projects (Build It Yourself) (2011) Donna Latham

Geek Toys Guide: Make a Real Light Saber and 64 Other Amazing Geek Toys (2013) Doug Cantor (editor)

Green Technology (Young Entrepreneurs Club) (2013) Mike Hobbs

Hands on Design and Technology (2011) Hilary Ansell

Ready Steady Origami: Over 40 Fun Paper Folding Projects (2010) Didier Boursin

Robotics: Discover the Science & Technology of the Future with 20 Projects (Build It Yourself) (2012) Kathy Ceceri

Technology For Fun (2011) Caroline Alliston

Winning Design! LEGO MINDSTORMS NXT Design Patterns for Fun and Competition (2010) James Trobaugh

Engineering

Bridges & Tunnels: Investigate Feats of Engineering with 25 Projects (Build It Yourself) (2012) Donna Latham

Canals & Dams: Investigate Feats of Engineering with 25 Projects (Build It Yourself) (2013) Donna Latham and Andrew Christensen

Cool Engineering Activities for Girls (Girl's Science Club) (2012) Heather Schwartz

Getting Started with Lego Robots: A Guide for K-12 Educators (2011) Mark Gura

If I Were an Engineer (2011) American Society for Engineering Education (author and publisher) Introducing engineering to 5-8 year olds

Making Things Move: DIY Mechanisms for Inventors, Hobbyists, and Artists (2011) Dustyn Roberts

Pop-Up: A Paper Engineering Master Class (2010) Ruth Wickings and Frances Castle

The Art of LEGO Mindstorms NXT-G Programming (2010) Terry Griffin

Maths

50 Amazing Things Kids Need to Know About Maths (50 Things Kids Need to Know) (2011) Anne Rooney

Amazing Math Projects You Can Build Yourself: Numbers, Geometry, Shapes (Build It Yourself) (2010) Laszlo Bardos and Samuel Carbaugh

Hello World! Computer Programming for Kids and Other Beginners (2013) Warren Sande and Carter Sande

How Many Socks Make a Pair? Surprisingly Interesting Maths (2011) Rob Eastaway

Math + Fashion = Fun: Move to the Head of the Class with Math Puzzles to Help You Pass! (2012) Aubre Andrus

Math Projects (2011) Joyce Stulgis-Blalock, Mary Dieterich and Sarah M. Anderson

Professor Stewart's Cabinet of Mathematical Curiosities (2010) Ian Stewart

Twitter

One of the fastest and easiest ways to keep up to date with resources is to use Twitter. Following carefully selected organisations or people allows you to read posts of interest. The limited number of characters in posts is not a problem as links can take you to more in-depth information. There is a growing appreciation that Twitter can be an excellent source of professional development, e.g. Needham (2013), @viciascience.

Once you have a Twitter account (via www.Twitter.com), then following some of the Twitter 'handles' of the organisations and people given below should make a useful start.

General STEM

@AAUWSTEM	@afterschool4all	@bisgovuk
@changeequation	@CLOtC	@CRESTAwards
@crest_star	@evecracker	@Future_Morph
@GeneratingG	@inthezone2012	@iom3
@mindsets_uk	@NtlSTEMCentre	@ORBITSTEM
@sciencecampaign	@STEMclubs	@STEMConnector
@STEMfinity	@stemnet	@STEM_Outreach
@STEM_Works	@TeachingSTEM	@TheEDTUK

Science

@theASE	@ASTA_online	@bridgetoscience
@BritishEcolSoc	@BritSciAssociat	@CLEAPSS
@DoTryThisAtHome	@DrAliceRoberts	@esa
@guardianscience	@HarryKroto	@imascientist
@jimalkhalili	@NASA	@NSTA
@PhysicsNews	@physorg_com	@ri_science
@RogerHighfield	@royalsociety	@RSC_EiC
@schoolscience	@ScienceVoice	@senseaboutsci
@Society_Biology	@TakeOnPhysics	@tesScience

Technology

@BBCClick	@BBCTech	@centre_alt_tech
@Cracking_Ideas	@DavidBarlex	@designcouncil
@DesignMuseum	@DTassoc	@firstlegoleague
@greentechnolog	@guardiantech	@IncredThings
@inhabitat	@Intelinvolved	@iom3
@julieboydonline	@make	@Next_Gadgets
@PracticalAction	@SmartPlanet	@techreview
@TechInSchool	@TechnologyUK	@TheGadgetShow

Engineering

@IEEESpectrum	@IEEEorg	@IETFaraday
@iteea	@ecomagination	@EduRAEng
@EliteEngUk	@egfi	@EngCareers
@engineer4change	@engineerinsight	@engineersworld
@EngtheFuture	@FLLUK	@ICE_engineers
@IMechE	@NACME	@RobotEvents
@Siemens_Energy	@SmallpeiceTrust	@thinkpoweruk
@TryEngineering	@VEXRobotics	@Young_Engineers

Maths

@4x4inSchools	@alexbellos	@atmaths
@CensusAtSchool	@CompAtSch	@IMAmaths
@maanow	@MarcusduSautoy	@Mathematical_A
@mathchat	@MathforAmerica	@MathsBusking
@Mathscareers	@mathshistory	@mathsinthecity
@MEImaths	@MMPmaths	@MoMath1
@Naace	@NCETM	@NCTM
@nrichmaths	@numberphile	@plusmathsorg
@rigb_maths	@RoyalStatSoc	@RSSCSE
@tesMaths	@UKMathsTrust	@virtualschooluk

Twitter is also useful for specific searches. The hash symbol (#) is used to tag topics, e.g. #stemclubs brings up posts about STEM clubs. Hashtags are also used to find posts, often about resources, generated by specific online meetings such as #ASEChat, #mathchat and #scichat.

Case Study 2.1, Organelle Wars, in Chapter 2 shows how Twitter can be used to extend and enhance lessons. The students in this example ended up with many relevant resources.

Chapter 10

Going further

Ideas from beyond the UK

By the end of this chapter, you will have ideas about how to:

- use successful STEM learning and teaching from beyond the UK to enrich lessons and extracurricular activities.

Successful STEM learning and teaching beyond the UK in lessons and beyond

Many of the challenges and opportunities for STEM educators are global issues. By looking at different approaches to learning and teaching about STEM used in schools across the world, many valuable ideas and approaches to supplement existing practices can be discovered.

When deciding whether successful strategies used in other schools, states or countries will work as well for you, some background describing their context can be useful. In the examples used in this chapter, information is given to help you make informed decisions about whether they are appropriate, in whole or in part, for immediate use or whether they are targets for the future.

The examples of international STEM events and activities given are chosen to illustrate further STEM enrichment and enhancement. Ways to use ideas from these international examples in UK classrooms, laboratories and workshops are suggested; with a little creativity, you could find many other ideas from the resources.

STEM activities from around the world

Some STEM clubs operate successfully with programmes of individual and even disconnected activities. These are often popular with students because they offer lots of different topics and are often associated with 'whiz, bang, splat' short activities that have immediate impact and high entertainment value. Examples include:

- making model volcanoes
- exploring crumple zones using eggs as crash dummies
- making an 'orchestra' out of fruit and vegetables.

Sourcing ideas to maintain programmes of this sort has been made relatively easy by the sharing of ideas from club leaders, and by accessing the resources webpages of museums, companies, government agencies and professional STEM subject associations.

Education resources that are particularly useful for STEM Club Programmes often accompany national projects and major events. One example from the UK includes the wide range of materials produced in the build-up to the 2012 Olympics. The legacy resources are available from the National STEM Centre eLibrary, filed under 'Olympic-and-Paralympic-games'. Resources such as these can be adapted for use as club activities or used within lessons to illustrate how the topics apply 'in the real world'.

The wide range of educational resources provided by the UK government Meteorological Office can also be used to show how STEM works, as there are short interactive games, longer puzzles and activities, suggestions for design-and-build projects and access to data sets to study weather records and atmospheric data in detail.

Earlier chapters, especially Chapters 3, 5 and 9, mention some examples of international projects and activities. The different examples given in Table 10.1 have been chosen for their particularly rich range of resources, most of which can be adapted for a wide age range of students.

Table 10.1 Examples of international projects with useful education resources

Project	Resources
National Aeronautics and Space Administration (NASA) (http://www.nasa.gov/offices/ education/about/index.html)	• Classroom activities • Videos • Interactive resources • Support for teachers • Recommended weblinks for more information
Conseil Européen pour la Recherche Nucléaire (CERN) (education.web.cern.ch)	• Lesson plans and resources • Information about how to access educational programmes, guided tours and summer schools for students and teachers
Incorporated Research Institutions for Seismology (IRIS) (http://www.iris.edu/hq/programs/ education_and_outreach)	• Monitor global earthquakes in near real time • Animations of seismic activity • Short video lectures • Lessons and resources
US Global Change Research Progamme (USGCRP) (http://www.globalchange.gov/ resources/educators)	• Climate Literacy Framework (available in English and Spanish) • Energy Literacy Framework • Teach Climate Literacy and Energy Awareness Network (CLEAN) • Reviewed educational resources • Wildlife and Wildlands Toolkit (for US locations) • Image gallery

United Nations Educational, Scientific and Cultural Organization (UNESCO) (http://www.unesco.org/archives/ multimedia)	• Audio and video material
	• Photographs and other resources. Topics include:
	  ○ Health education
	  ○ Education for sustainable development

Mathematics of Planet Earth (http://mpe2013.org)	Available in English, French and Spanish • Biodiversity • Modelling disease • Ecology • Epidemiology • Ocean • Transportation

Most of the resources in Table 10.1 extend to include all the STEM subjects. For example, Technology links to:

- space research
- new Smart materials, byproducts of space research
- building the Large Hadron Collider at CERN
- buildings that withstand earthquakes
- monitoring climate change
- sustainable building design
- transportation.

The growing ranges of statistics, which can be accessed from national organisations, are proving to be extremely useful sources of data for use in schools. Unexpected facts or figures can be used to stimulate critical thinking about topics. Authentic data can allow students to explore curriculum topics in depth.

In the UK, sets of environmental data are available from the Department for Environment, Food and Rural Affairs (DEFRA). These focus on food, farming, environment, wildlife and the countryside. The statistical information available from DEFRA is a rich source of stimulus materials for across-STEM lessons.

For example, a chart showing the proportions of domestic waste recycled or sent to landfill over the past decade could be used in Maths to support arguments about the country's capacity to meet the European Union's target of 50 per cent waste recycled by 2020. In Design & Technology the historical impact of changing product packaging could be explored from the data and challenges set to design yet greener packaging. In Science the relative degradation times of different materials could be investigated as well as issues associated with environmental contamination from landfill sites.

A contrasting source of rich data is available from the National Center for Health Statistics (US) website, particularly the 'Data & Statistics' section. From the NCHS website it is possible to interrogate data about a diverse range of health topics. For example, students could:

- look at annual statistics
- explore variations in the data over a period of time
- investigate the trends in the number of adults with diabetes per US state over the past 15 years
- compare trends in adult obesity with the trends in diabetes over the same period
- analyse information from the 'obesity risk atlas'
- download a slide show of the historical data (search for obesity trends 2010 PowerPoint) to extract material for their own presentation.

Not only does engagement with data in this way bring realism and authenticity to the study of curriculum topics, it can stimulate students to devise projects to explore subjects further.

Some countries, such as the USA and Canada, have many schools with the tradition of including students' projects in their annual school calendar. In these educational systems, students build up the necessary skills to complete meaningful projects through preparatory experiences that are built into their curriculum. The projects shared through websites normally focus on the subject of the project and not the prior experience of the participants, so it is up to you to 'read between the lines' in order to decide whether similar projects would fit, unmodified, into your programmes.

With tight constraints on curriculum time, some staff may be tempted to regard student project work as a luxury for only engaging with in extracurricular time. This is not necessarily the case, as with a bit of flexible thinking, 'traditional' STEM subject areas can be taught through contemporary examples.

Topics such as recycling, home insulation, sustainable fishing and pollution could be taught using resources from the International Polar Foundation (IPF). In many cases these can be used as direct substitutes for existing materials in schools, challenging any objections that there is not enough time in the curriculum for projects or problem-based learning. For example, information from the IPF's Sustainable Fishing resources, via their educational website, EducaPoles, could be used during the curriculum topic 'human impact on the environment' or when looking at food webs or predator–prey relationships. The background materials also have sufficient detail for interested students to explore the topics as projects in extracurricular time.

Clearly there are advantages in using resources from international bodies such as the IPF. The Science and associated economic, social and political issues are instantly placed in a real-life example. The website, which has English, French and Dutch language versions, also includes additional information which could be used by students as the basis for projects of their own. Some sample projects are also included on the website.

International study visits

Although still not commonplace, and often reserved for older students, STEM study visits to other countries are growing in popularity. There are wonderful opportunities for students and teachers to travel to amazing destinations to carry out STEM projects or visit internationally renowned institutions such as CERN in Switzerland. Some organisations offer sponsorship for major visits like these; the alternative is to plan ahead and fundraise. Chapter 7 has advice about risk assessments; Chapter 8 has ideas for fundraising.

The benefits of such visits may include students:

- studying new examples of biological diversity not available in the school vicinity, for example in locations with different temperature and humidity ranges or different altitudes
- exploring first-hand the geological features associated with other landscapes
- finding out more about the impact of the extraction of raw materials, for example, mining for the minerals needed for computer chips
- discovering the ways that cultures adapt technologies or develop alternative solutions to meet their needs.

Study visits abroad do not necessarily have time built in for students to meet and work with other students from the country being visited. This may be because it is a period of school holiday for both the visiting students and those in the host country, or there may simply not be sufficient time in the visit agenda. The next section looks at how students from schools in different countries can collaborate.

International school collaboration

Just as learning can be stimulated by curriculum examples from around the world, students can learn from each other by exchanging information about lifestyles, environments and views on a variety of issues. The STEM subjects have a lot to gain from linking up with schools from different countries; comparisons of diet or design of their respective school buildings can support student discussions across the STEM subjects and potentially stimulate project work.

The range of ways in which schools and individual students can exchange information has expanded rapidly with the facilities possible through the World Wide Web. Whilst emails are still a useful way to transfer data files, access to other more interactive platforms supports sharing and working collaboratively on presentations as well as holding discussions and even debates via video links.

Schools have a responsibility to keep students safe and each school should have cyber security precautions in place. These may limit the options available for collaboration and information exchange information with other schools. The benefits to students of being involved in international collaboration are so profound that it is worth STEM teachers taking time to find out what communication methods are possible within the school cyber security regulations.

Clearly, internet links offer valuable means of students communicating with each other, but students' learning experiences will be all the richer if they can take part in some form of visit programme and spend time in each other's communities.

The most common type of visit programme is having 'exchange' or reciprocated visits by staff and students between partnered or 'twinned' schools. This practice usually takes place in UK schools through student exchange programmes organised by staff from Modern Languages departments but the process could have a much wider remit with visits regarded as whole school learning opportunities.

Finding exchange partners to engage in collaborative learning projects or to carry out reciprocal study visits can be progressed by:

- using personal contacts
- following up recommendations, e.g. from colleagues working abroad
- joining groups of schools recruited for an international project, e.g. projects sponsored by the British Council or those funded through the European Union through the Comenius Project
- using online linking services to locate participating schools fitting your preferred parameters. Table 10.2 gives information about some school linking services, all of which are free for schools.

Table 10.2 School linking services

Linking service	Brief information, including quotes from some of the linking service websites
eTwinning	Free for all European schools
	'It is not about creating extra work, but providing a framework for exciting curriculum work with partners in another country'
British Council Schools online	Free to all schools globally
	'This website offers resources and project templates you can use in your partnerships'
Science Across the World Facebook group	Group established by Science Across the World enthusiasts, so a 'self-help' group offering support to new teachers (see Chapter 5)
FACTWorld	Run by volunteer teachers
	'FACTWorld is a forum set up to support the teaching of subjects through the medium of foreign language, bilingual education, immersion education, content and language integrated learning'

Irrespective of the means by which a school exchange is secured, it is important to plan for meaningful engagements between students while they are in STEM subject or club time. This may mean even more than usual use of 'show stopping' demonstrations or spending time on activities which are well supported by video tutorials or well-illustrated instruction sheets. These sorts of approach will minimise the need to refer to technical terms in oral instructions as these could be beyond the language skills of visiting students, so discouraging them from participating fully in the activities. With advance planning between the STEM staff in the exchange schools, the visiting students could prepare and present some information about themselves and their interests in STEM to the host students, perhaps led by their teacher to help overcome any nervousness.

Case Study 10.1 shows how one school enhanced its STEM enrichment programme by integrating STEM-based activities into a school exchange programme.

CASE STUDY 10.1   **Exchanging information about STEM projects between students from partnered exchange schools**

A rural secondary school in the UK had a strong commitment to learning for sustainable development. Staff and pupils were actively involved in the Eco-Schools network.

A funding opportunity allowed the school to invest in growing 'elephant grass' (*Miscanthus* sp.) as a biofuel as part of the school's contribution to a newly established community sustainable energy project.

To deepen its 'learning for sustainability' commitment, the school deliberately searched for potential exchange partner schools with similar principles. It was successful in securing 'twinning' relationships with a school in Scandinavia, which used electricity generated from hydroelectric sources, and a school in Iceland which used geothermal energy. Having the opportunity to exchange information with these partner schools provided much more realism to the delivery of the related areas in the STEM curriculum as well as contributing to the school's sustainability ethos.

When the students from the UK visited their exchange schools they took part in specially prepared activities to help them learn more about how the host schools' energy needs were met. They also learned about the construction methods used to build the schools, and where the materials were sourced. These activities took up a relatively small amount of the visit, so there was plenty of time left for other educational, cultural and social activities; but their impact was long-standing, and certainly added greatly to the overall success of the exchange visit.

In preparation for their turn to act as hosts for visits by the partner schools, STEM students from the UK school devised a walking tour to show off various features of their school and the town it served. Their tour included a visit to the fields where the elephant grass was growing and later they shared images from a video diary showing how the fields were prepared for planting (and made sheep-proof!) and how the grass was processed after harvesting.

Subsequently members of the school STEM club created a presentation for sharing information about their project at a West Midlands STEMNET conference convened to help share and celebrate the project work of STEM clubs in the region.

The school continues to have eco credentials and has a legacy of continuing opportunities for collaboration with the established exchange partner schools. Much of the original STEM tour is still incorporated into visit programmes, so new generations of students are benefitting from the experiences.

Invitation to extend your expertise further

We have been privileged over the past decade or so to observe and share in some truly outstanding examples of STEM enrichment and enhancement activities. Our passion and determination to bring such activities into the lives of as many students as possible have brought us to writing this book.

The origins of the STEM agenda have been described, including the need for STEM literacy for all citizens. Ideas for enhancing and enriching STEM lessons have been given as well as advice on setting up and running STEM clubs successfully. How to get more students interested in STEM careers has been discussed and teachers supported with advice on health and safety issues, funding and where to find resources, including from overseas.

We have given many examples of rich STEM learning experiences for you to use with your students. We hope that we have also given you insights into new ways and means to extend your current practice.

The impact of your successful delivery of STEM activities will be reflected in the future achievements of your students.

Chapter 11

Ideas bank

Projects and activities for all ages

Many of the examples given here could be used for activities or projects for most ages of students, just tackled at different depths. In Table 11.1, simpler activities, perhaps more suitable for younger students, or as pilot activities, are given first, followed by ideas for extension projects or activities.

The 'basic projects' listed in the table all come from real activities or projects carried out by students. Some are therefore given as research questions; others are not.

They come from a variety of sources, including:

1   STEM Challenges (archived)
2   CREST Award titles
3   Websites recommending or celebrating successful projects such as:
    a   OPAL surveys
    b   The Mathematical Association of America's Math Club
    c   Young Engineers
    d   STEM club network ideas
    e   Other.

The numbers in brackets, after the titles, link to the above list to identify the source. To find more details for titles from sources 1–3d, use Chapter 9. Weblinks are given for titles from sources 3e. If any no longer work, try searching the home page of the website using key words.

Topics are arranged under STEM, Science, Technology, Engineering and Maths. However, some could be used in other categories, so it is worth checking outside your area of interest.

Table 11.1 Ideas for STEM projects and activities for students of all ages

STEM

Basic project	Possible extension
Research, design and make minibeast 'hotels' (3d)	Monitor how the new 'hotel' is populated and naturalised into its environment
Build your own ejector seat and balloon hovercraft (3e): http://www.bbc.co.uk/bbcone/wallaceandgromit/hands-on	Add a 'passenger' to the ejector seat and design a parachute to ensure the passenger lands safely
Space camp STEM day (3d)	Plan a visit to the National Space Centre in Leicester

Crazy golf design day (3d)	Design and make a challenging crazy golf hole or holes to use as an activity at a school fair
Ballista challenge (3d)	Arrange a visit from the Young Archaeologists Club (YAC) or try some of the activities suggested on the YAC website (www.yac-uk.org)
Chocolate welding (3d)	Follow up with a more quantitative challenge using ideas from 'Engineering with Chocolate' from Tomorrow's Engineers (www.tomorrowsengineers.org.uk)
Light stitches – use textiles and electronics to make products (3e) (http://www.stemclubs.net/activity/2982/light_stitches)	Vote on the most commercial product made and produce more to sell; profits could be used for more club activities
Glow in the dark workshop (3d)	Find a specialist who can provide a lecture to the members about natural luminescence
Build a model fairground waltzer system that measures the force on passengers (3d)	Take club members on a trip to a theme park; most have educational resources to download in preparation for the visit
Forge the Mona Lisa: students produce a copy of the Mona Lisa that would pass as many chemical analysis techniques as possible (3d)	Arrange a visit from an art restorer or a local auctioneer, or a forensic expert to talk about detecting forgeries

Science

Basic project	Possible extension
Is the size of a pond related to its aquatic diversity? (3a)	Compare the ponds at different times of the year Calculate indices of diversity
Do different habitat types have different soil pH values? (3a)	Consider implications of local soil pH values on choice of crops to be cultivated for a 'Grow and Cook' initiative
Do neatly trimmed hedges house fewer invertebrates than hedges not cut so frequently? (3a)	Extend into a longitudinal study Compare results with those found by students in a school with different hedges
What is the best liquid cleaning product, shampoo, liquid soap or washing-up liquid for washing hair? (2)	Extend investigation to compare effects of different conditioners on the appearance and strength of hair
Use a version of Archimedes' method to investigate the composition of copper, silver and gold items (2)	Investigate using electrolysis to electroplate materials
Does the fastest speed of a tennis serve depend on the player's height? (3e) (http://www.planet-science.com/categories/over-11s/human-body/2011/06/does-the-fastest-tennis-serve-depend-on-height.aspx)	Investigate the 'sweet spot' on a tennis racket Use video editing software to track a moving tennis ball and calculate its speed

(continued)

Table 11.1 (continued)

Science

Basic project	Possible extension
Use chromatography to detect forged cheques and other documents and various types of counterfeit goods (2)	Find out how watermarks are embedded into bank notes
	Explore inks and dyes that fluoresce under ultraviolet light
Fireworks – indoor fireworks, making sparklers and flame tests (3d)	Make rocket-propelled model cars – see the education pages of the Bloodhound SSC website for more information (http://www. bloodhoundssc.com/education)
Investigate how velocity and other factors affect the extent of bodywork damage in head-on collisions between model vehicles (2)	Find out about the use of crash dummies for vehicle safety tests
	Design a working model of a vehicle air bag and demonstrate it working

Technology

Basic project	Possible extension
Investigate and suggest a 'waste-free' lunch programme for your school (3e) (http://www.epa.gov/osw/education/lunch.htm)	Work with members of the school Eco committee to explore other waste reduction possibilities around school
Belching bins and clucking cups (3e): (http://www.csiro.au/helix/sciencemail/activities/cluckcup.html)	Research and make thunder drums or rainmaker tubes
Jewellery design workshop (3d)	Build in some ultraviolet-reacting beads to indicate when the wearer has been exposed to sunlight for a period of time
The Great Egg Race (3e): (http://www.bbc.co.uk/archive/great_egg_race)	Devise a set of rules to make your favourite egg race into an inter-form competition
Tallest jelly competition (3d)	Explore how the enzymes in some fresh fruits such as pineapple prevent jellies from setting
Present proposals for efficient and effective ways to light the playing area within a new National Handball Centre, with a suggested design for the court, including floor material (1)	Use Google Sketchup to make three-dimensional drawings of proposed handball centre
Compare how well bread rises when made from different types of flour (2)	Compare the effects of making the same bread mixtures by hand and using a bread-making machine
Design an electronic circuit that makes Christmas tree lights flash automatically (2)	Add suitable sensors and timer so that the Christmas tree lights switch on whenever someone is near and go off when the person moves away
Processing a fleece (3d)	Observe the texture of the fleece with a microscope. If possible, compare fleece from different breeds of sheep
Design and build a working speaker system (2)	Investigate the effect of the position of the speaker system within a room on the quality of the sound

Engineering

Basic project	Possible extension
Model the construction of a sports arena (1)	Invite a member of the local Fire Authority to brief the club or class about fire safety regulations for large facilities like an arena
Build a model pirate ship ride (2)	Develop the model so that it is self-powered
Make Solar boats (3d)	Extend the project to make amphibian vehicles
Barbie-Bob skeleton testing (3d)	Evaluate different test surfaces for a bob skeleton course to find the fastest
Build jelly bean towers (3d)	Make a shake table to test the towers for resistance to earthquakes
Buildings come in all shapes and sizes, and can be modest or extravagant. Your challenge is to present proposals for a structure for a national handball centre. You should also suggest the materials to be used (1)	Research and design a version of the handball centre that does not include any imported building materials or other products
Investigate air-conditioning systems used on trains (2)	Find out about heat recovery systems and whether these could be incorporated
Make a stored-power vehicle to set size limitations from suitable materials, to beat competitors (3c)	Compare the efficiencies of different designs on flat surfaces and on inclines
Build a super dome (http://teachers.egfi-k12.org/design-a-super-dome)	Construct a model of the biomes at the Eden Project
Investigate the Bloodhound air-powered dragster (3d)	Move on to one of the other Bloodhound challenges, like breaking the model rocket-powered car speed record

Mathematics

Basic project	Possible extension
Create a scale model of a racing boat (1)	Create a scale model of the school and/or grounds
How does the height of a rollercoaster track affect the speed of a car on the ride? (2)	Investigate the effect of different numbers of passengers in the car. Does where they sit in the car affect the results?
Snake coil challenge (3b)	Produce an animation to illustrate your answer to the challenge
Bead bracelet challenge (3b)	Investigate designs of bead bracelets from different cultures
Cafeteria survey: what is the best way to fit in all the tables? (3b)	Is best really best? Compare the mathematical solution for the most efficient way to place tables and chairs in the cafeteria with students' views about the most welcoming space to eat

(continued)

Table 11.1 (continued)

Mathematics	
Basic project	*Possible extension*
Pi Day with Pie Projects. Circle measurement, circumference and area computation to irrationality and how to calculate and approximate the value of pi (3b)	Carry out practical work on circles and segments in a Design & Technology room, so you can eat the ingredients you have been working with
Present proposals for a new national handball (or sport of choice) centre, with a scale drawing of the outline floor plan, including suggested spectator seating arrangements (1)	Investigate the effects of scaling up or down the floor plan of the construction on the total spectator capacity
Participate in a World Wide Web mathematical scavenger hunt. Have the students look for additional problem resources, formula pages, pages about pi, e, the golden ratio, mathematical bloopers and fallacies (3b)	Work as a group to produce a school mathematical scavenger hunt suitable for visiting students from a feeder school
Horse racing, chance and probability (http://www.australiancurriculumlessons.com.au/2012/10/08/horse-racing-probability-and-chance)	Contact the British Horseracing Education and Standards Trust to arrange a visit to a local race track to see how maths is applied
Dice football competition (http://www.australiancurriculumlessons.com.au/2012/12/02/dice-football-part-2-competition-design)	Look at variations on first past the post, knock-out and round robin sports tournaments used for major sports. Do these relate to the physical demands of the sports involved or to the best returns for event sponsors?
Secret codes and ciphers (3d)	Consider visiting Bletchley Park, the National Codes and Cipher Centre. If not possible, register for an Enigma Outreach visit (http://www.bletchleypark.org.uk/edu/visit/outreach.rhtm)

Glossary

STEM Acronym for Science, Technology, Engineering and Mathematics

STEM agenda A range of reports and subsequent initiatives, targets and action plans drawn up and implemented to meet the projected needs of industry and associated academia. A complex concept! See Chapter 1

STEM ambassadors Valuable, free human resources for UK teachers and schools. Ambassadors with a STEM background volunteer to help with clubs, competitions, careers talks, lessons and more, with the aim of inspiring pupils about STEM subjects

To find an ambassador in your region, see: www.stemnet.org.uk/contact

To become an ambassador, see: db.stemnet.org.uk/register.cfm

STEM clubs Any club that links to a STEM area. May be single-focus, e.g. robotics or chess club, or may encompass a wider variety of STEM areas – all are called STEM clubs

Complement the curriculum with activities that may involve practical experiments, investigation, discussion and reflection. And are fun

For those who struggle with STEM subjects and for those who need extension and enrichment opportunities

STEM club advisor Person who supports the delivery of the STEM clubs network projects in 11–18-years schools across England. Likely to work with partners, including STEMNET, the Association for Science Education and the Network of Regional Science Learning Centres

STEM clubs network UK network, coordinated by STEMNET

Online help, support, advice, examples, case studies, resources, guides, ideas for activities and more (http://www.stemclubs.net)

STEM clubs programme Extended 2012–2013 to cover all parts of the UK

Run by STEMNET until at least 2015. Supported by the Gatsby Charitable Foundation and the Department for Education

STEM contract holder One of 45 sub-regional contract holders in the UK who help STEMNET deliver its programmes to schools and organisations in their local area, through the STEM ambassador programme and the Schools STEM Advisory Network

STEM coordinator A staff role, usually in an 11–18-years school, that carries responsibility for overseeing and coordinating STEM activities within school. May have time allowance or salary scale points

STEM Directories   Created in direct response to teachers' needs. Comprise an online collection of schemes and activities provided by organisations from across the UK to enhance and enrich the curriculum

www.stemdirectories.org.uk/about_us.cfm

www.stemdirectories.org.uk/teacher-faqs

STEM literacy   Understanding scientific, technological and mathematical ideas, applications and implications and being able to use these in everyday life

STEM Manager tool   Free, online resource available from the National STEM Centre to help plan an integrated approach to STEM in school

STEMNET   A national organisation funded by the Department for Business, Innovation and Skills, managed locally by sub-regional partners. There are 45 sub-regional partners in the UK who help STEMNET deliver free programmes to schools and organisations in their local area, through the STEM ambassador programme and the Schools STEM Advisory Network

STEM programme   Various meanings since the phrase was coined. Generally applies to an intentional combination of services, events and opportunities, including training opportunities, which collectively further the aims of the STEM agenda for a chosen target audience

References

Abrahams, I. and Millar, R. (2008) Does practical work really work? A study of the effectiveness of practical work as a teaching and learning method in school science. *International Journal of Science Education*, 30(14): 1945–1969.

Abrahams, I. and Reiss, M. (2012) Practical work: its effectiveness in primary and secondary schools in England. *Journal of Research into Science Teaching*, 49(8): 1035–1055.

Abrahams, I., Braund, M. and Saglam, M. (2011) *Performing Science: Teaching Chemistry, Physics and Biology Through Drama and Role Play*. London: Continuum.

Afterschool Alliance (2013) *Defining Youth Outcomes for STEM Learning in Afterschool*. Available online at: http://www.afterschoolalliance.org.

Archer, L., Osborne, J. and DeWitt, J. (2012) *Ten Science Facts and Fictions: The Case for Early Education about STEM Careers*. London: The Science Council.

Arnold, C. (2010) Low-grade science: primary school students conduct and publish a study on bees. *Scientific American*, 21 December. Available online at: http://www.scientificamerican.com/article.cfm?id=low-grade-science-primary-school.

ASPIRES project (2009) Available online at: https://www.kcl.ac.uk/sspp/departments/education/research/aspires/index.aspx.

Association for Science Education (2001) *Topics in Safety*, 3rd edn. Hatfield: Association for Science Education.

Association for Science Education (2006) *Safeguards in the School Laboratory*, 11th edn. Hatfield: Association for Science Education.

Association for Science Education (2007) Oh yes you can: safety matters. *Education in Science*, 224: 27.

Association for Science Education (2010) *Safe and Exciting Science*, 2nd edn. Hatfield: Association for Science Education.

Association for Science Education Chat (2012) *How Do You Run a Successful Science Club?* ASE chat summary 72. Available online at: http://www.ase.org.uk/documents/ase-chat-summary-72.

Aston Business School (2012) *Global Enterprise Monitor Press Release*. Available online at: http://www1.aston.ac.uk/about/news/releases/2012/august/uk-business-start-up.

Back, J. and Lee, T. (2003) *Dramatic Mathematics*. Available online at: http://nrich.maths.org/2433.

Baker, Y. (2013) *Yvonne Baker On Careers Advice – A Response To Telegraph's Brian Cox Interview*. Available online at: http://sciencelearningcentres.wordpress.com/tag/science-teaching-2.

Barmby, P., Kind, P. and Jones, K. (2008) Examining changing attitudes in secondary school science. *International Journal of Science Education*, 30(8): 1075–1093.

BBC (2013) *Data Protection Act*. Available online at: http://www.bbc.co.uk/schools/gcsebitesize/ict/legal/0dataprotectionactrev1.shtml.

Beddington, J. and Rothwell, N. (2012) STEM Education. *Text of a letter to the Prime Minister*. Available online at: http://www.bis.gov.uk/assets/cst/docs/files/letters/12-1272-stem-education-letter-to-prime-minister.pdf.

Be ENGinious. Available online at: http://www.setpointherts.org.uk/#/stem-clubs/4540621131.

Beyond Current Horizons (2009) *Educational, Social and Technological Futures: Final Report*. Available online at: http://www.beyondcurrenthorizons.org.uk/outcomes.

Biochemical Society (2009) *Hive 9, A Play about Evolution*. Available online at: http://www.biochemistry.org/Education/Events/Outreach/TheDarwinProject.aspx.

Blackawton, P.S. *et al.* (2010) Blackawton bees. Available online at: http://rsbl.royalsocietypublishing.org/site/misc/BlackawtonBees.xhtml

Blackawton, P.S. *et al.* (2011) Blackawton bees. Biology Letters (Royal Society), 7(2): 168–172.

Blatchford, R. (2013) *How Teachers Can Show Student Progress During Lesson Observations*. Available online at: http://www.sec-ed.co.uk/best-practice/how-teachers-can-show-visible-progress-when-they-are-being-observed.

Borrows, P. (2006) Chemistry outdoors. *School Science Review*, 87(320): 23–31.

Bridges, A. (2012) *Extra! Extra! Read All About Science: Teachers and Experts Share Their Secrets on Using the News to Enrich Science Classes*. Available online at: http://www.sciencenewsforkids.org/2012/07/extra-extra-read-all-about-science.

British Society for the History of Science (2011) *Object Stories*. Available online at: http://www.bshs.org.uk/object-stories.

British Standards Institution (2007) *Health and Safety for Design and Technology in Schools and Similar Establishments: Code of Practice*, 5th edn, vol. 4163., viii, 131. London: British Standards Institution.

Brough, J. (1859) *Fairy Tales of Science*. London: Griffith and Farran.

Carter, E. (2012) Be inspired, inspire others. *School Science Review*, 94(346): 27–32.

Carter, E. (2013) A treasure hunt through time and space. *School Science Review*, 95(348): 16–26.

Chapman, S. and Smith, A. (2007) 21st century science clubs: enhancing the curriculum. *School Science Review*, 89(327): 83–89.

Chevalier, T. (2010) *Remarkable Creatures*. London: Harper.

Clarke, J. (2013) *Shining a Light on Solar Power and Renewable Energy in Your Classroom*. Guardian online, Teacher Network. Available online at: http://www.guardian.co.uk/teacher-network/teacher-blog/2013/jan/15/solar-power-renewable-energy-green-schools?CMP=new_53&j=26291&e=howarthsg@yahoo.co.uk&l=187_HTML&u=1334316&mid=1059027&jb=1&CMP=.

Clarke, P., Howarth, S., Whitehouse, K. and Wood-Griffiths, S. (2012) Perspectives on teacher education. Risk-taking in the workplace; challenging trainee teachers to develop their practice. *At the Crossroads: New Directions in Teacher Education*. Canterbury Christ Church University, Faculty of Education, Jubilee Conference. Abstract available online at: http://www.canterbury.ac.uk/education/new-directions/docs/abstracts.pdf, p. 24.

CLEAPSS (1998) *Developing and Using Environmental Areas in School Grounds*. L221. Available online at: http://www.cleapss.org.uk/attachments/article/0/L221.pdf?Primary/Resources/Guides.

CLEAPSS (2006a) *Practical Activities in the School Grounds etc*. SRA 08. Available online at: http://www.cleapss.org.uk/attachments/article/0/SRA08.pdf?Secondary/Science/Supp%27%20risk%20assessments/#search=%22SRA%2008%22.

CLEAPSS (2006b) *Running a Prep Room*. L248a. Available online at: http://www.cleapss.org.uk/attachments/article/0/L248A.pdf?Secondary/Science/Guides/#search=%22CLEAPSS%202006b%20L248a%20Running%20a%20Prep%20Room%22.

CLEAPPS (2006c) *Managing Risk Assessment in Design and Technology*. L235. Available online at: http://www.cleapss.org.uk/attachments/article/0/L235.pdf?Secondary/D&T%20and%20Art%20&%20Design/Guides/#search=%22CLEAPPS%202006c%20L235%20Managing%20Risk%20Assessment%20in%20Design%20and%20Technology%22.

CLEAPSS (2008) *Fireworks and Explosives*. PS 81. Available online at: http://www.cleapss.org.uk/attachments/article/0/PS81.pdf?Secondary/Science/Guidance%20

Leaflets/#search=%22CLEAPSS%202008%20PS%2081%20Fireworks%20and%20 Explosives%22.

CLEAPSS (2011) *REACH and the Teaching of Practical Chemistry*. Available online at: http://www. cleapss.org.uk/attachments/article/0/REACH.pdf?Free%20Publications/#search=%22CLEA PSS%202011%20REACH%20and%20the%20teaching%20of%20practical%20chemistry%22.

Cleaves, A. (2005) Formation of science choices in secondary school. *International Journal of Science Education*, 27(4): 471–486.

Confederation of British Industries (2011) *Report*. Available online at: http://www.cbi.org.uk/ media-centre/news-articles/2011/02/education-and-skills-survey-2011.

Confederation of British Industries (2012) *Report*. Available online at: http://www.national numeracy.org.uk/files/42/CBI%20Education%20and%20Skills%20survey%20-%20pub lished%20June%202012.pdf.

Consortium of Local Education Authorities for the Provision of Science Services (CLEAPSS) (1991) *Laboratory Handbook*. Section 17: Monitoring in the field and laboratory. Available online at: http://www.cleapss.org.uk/attachments/article/0/Preface.pdf?Secondary.

Council for Learning Outside the Classroom (2013a) Available online at: http://www.lotc.org. uk/category/research.

Council for Learnng Outside the Classroom (2013b) *Making Your Own Fieldguide for the School Grounds*. Available online at: http://www.lotc.org.uk/2013/01/making-your-own-fieldguide-for-the-school-grounds.

DATA (2008) *Risk Assessment in Secondary Schools and Colleges. Design & Technology Teaching Environments; Health and Safety Guidance*. Wellesbourne, Warwickshire: DATA.

DATA (2013) *FAQ*. Available online at: http://www.data.org.uk/index.php?option=com_ content&view=article&id=877&Itemid=696#age.

Department for Business, Innovation and Skills (2011) *The Returns to Higher Education Qualifications*. BIS research paper number 45. Available online at: https://www.gov.uk/ government/uploads/system/uploads/attachment_data/file/32419/11-973-returns-to-higher-education-qualifications.pdf.

Department for Education (2000–2009) *Licence to Cook Case Studies – Health and Safety*. Available online at: http://stem.org.uk/rx9n4.

Department for Education (2004) *STEM Mapping Review*. Available online at: http://www. nationalstemcentre.org.uk/elibrary/resource/4958/report-on-the-stem-mapping-review-2004.

Department for Education (2006) *Science, Technology, Engineering and Mathematics (STEM) Programme Report*. Available online at: http://www.nationalstemcentre.org.uk/ stem-programme/stem-background.

Department for Education (2011) *Maths and Science Education: The Supply of High Achievers at A Level*. Research Report DFE-RR079. Available online at: https://www.gov.uk/ government/uploads/system/uploads/attachment_data/file/182261/DFE-RR079. pdf.

Department for Education (2012a) *The English Baccalaureate*. Available online at: http://www. education.gov.uk/schools/teachingandlearning/qualifications/englishbac/a0075975/ the-english-baccalaureate.

Department for Education (2012b) *Departmental Advice on Health and Safety for Schools*. Available online at: http://www.education.gov.uk/aboutdfe/advice/f00191759/departmental-advice-on-health-and-safety-for-schools.

Department for Education (2012c) *The School Curriculum*. Available online at: http://www. education.gov.uk/schools/teachingandlearning/curriculum.

Department for Education (2013a) *Departmental Advice on Health and Safety for Schools*. Available online at: http://www.education.gov.uk/aboutdfe/advice/f00191759/departmental-advice-on-health-and-safety-for-schools.

Department for Education (2013b) *Statutory Guidance: The Duty to Secure Independent and Impartial Careers Guidance for Young People in Schools*. Available online at: http://media.

education.gov.uk/assets/files/pdf/s/careers%20guidance%20for%20schools%20-%20statu tory%20guidance%20-%20march%202013.pdf.

Department for Education (2013c) *GCSE and Equivalent Results in England 2011/12* (revised). Available online at: https://www.gov.uk/government/uploads/system/uploads/ attachment_data/file/219341/sfr02_202013.pdf.

Department for Education and Skills (2006) *The Science, Technology, Engineering and Mathematics (STEM) Programme Report*. Available online at: http://www.nationalstemcentre.org.uk/ res/documents/page/stem_programme_report_2006.pdf ISBN: 978-184478-827-9.

DeRusha, K. and Wolfson, B. (2010) *Teaching Engineering Using Dramatic Play*. Available online at: www.integratingengineering.org.

Disclosure and Barring Service (DBS) Available online at: http://www.homeoffice.gov.uk/ crime/vetting-barring-scheme.

Dohn, N. (2011) Situational interest of high school students who visit an aquarium. *Science Education*, 95(2): 337–357.

Donna, R. (2012) *Edible Printer Inks – Specially Formulated Food Coloring for Your Cakes*. Available online at: www.sooperarticles.com/technology-articles/hardware-articles/ edible-printer-inks-specially-formulated-food-coloring-your-cakes-1069477.html#ixzz 2J7ZN7ky0.

Drabble, E. (2011a) *How to Teach . . . The Winter Solstice*. Guardian online, Teacher Network. Available online at: http://www.guardian.co.uk/education/2011/dec/19/winter-solstice-teaching-sun-moon.

Drabble, E. (2011b) *How to Teach . . . National Tree Week*. Guardian online, Teacher Network. Available online at: http://www.guardian.co.uk/education/2011/nov/28/national-tree-week-teaching-resources.

Drabble, E. (2011c) *How to Teach . . . Children to Cook*. Guardian online, Teacher network. Available online at: http://www.guardian.co.uk/education/2011/oct/24/jamie-oliver-teaching-resources.

Drabble, E. (2011d) *How to Teach . . . Saving Energy*. Guardian online, Teacher Network. Available online at: http://www.guardian.co.uk/education/2011/oct/17/energy-consumption-renewables-lesson-plans.

Drabble, E. (2012a) *How to Teach . . . Gravity*. Guardian online, Teacher Network. Available online at: http://www.guardian.co.uk/education/2012/oct/22/how-to-teach-gravity-felix-baumgartner.

Drabble, E. (2012b) *How to Teach . . . World Food Day*. Guardian online, Teacher Network. Available online at: http://www.guardian.co.uk/education/2012/oct/08/world-food-day-school-resources.

Drabble, E. (2012c) *How to Teach . . . Polar Meltdown*. Guardian online, Teacher Network. Available online at: http://www.guardian.co.uk/education/2012/sep/17/polar-arctic-meltdown-climate-change.

Drabble, E. (2012d) *How to Teach . . . Mini-beasts*. Guardian online, Teacher Network. Available online at: http://www.guardian.co.uk/education/2012/jun/18/national-insect-week-teaching-resources.

Drabble, E. (2012e) *How to Teach . . . World Health Day*. Guardian online, Teacher Network. Available online at: http://www.guardian.co.uk/education/2012/apr/02/world-health-day-teaching-resources.

Drabble, E. (2012f) *How to Teach . . . Drought*. Guardian online, Teacher Network. Available online at: http://www.guardian.co.uk/education/2012/mar/26/teaching-resources-drought-uk-hosepipe.

Drabble, E. (2013) *How to Teach . . . Astronomy*. Guardian online, Teacher Network. Available online at: http://www.guardian.co.uk/education/teacher-blog/2013/jan/14/ astronomy-schools-teaching-resource.

Drury, E. (2012) *How to Launch an Environmental Project at Your School.* Guardian online, Teacher Network. Available online at: http://www.guardian.co.uk/teacher-network/2012/oct/01/how-to-launch-environmental-project-at-school?CMP=NLCJOBEML8714&CMP.

Education Scotland (2011) *The National Curriculum for Scotland.* Available online at: www.scotland.gov.uk/Topics/Education/Schools/curriculum.

EngineeringUK (2011a) *STEM Teacher Careers Information Survey: Summary of Key Findings.* Available online at: http://www.engineeringuk.com/_resources/documents/STEM_Teachers_Careers_Survey_Aug_2011.pdf.

EngineeringUK (2011b) *An Investigation into Why the UK Has the Lowest Proportion of Female Engineers in the EU. A Summary of the Key Issues.* Available online at: http://www.engineeringuk.com/_resources/documents/Int_Gender_summary_EngineeringUK_04_11_.pdf.

EngineeringUK (2011c) *Student Subject Decision Making Aged 14 and 16.* Available online at: http://www.engineeringuk.com/_resources/documents/Report_into_student_course_decision_making_aged_14_and_16.pdf.

Equal Opportunities Commission (2005) *Employers, Young People and Gender Segregation (England).* Available online at: http://www.equalityhumanrights.com/uploaded_files/sex_and_power_2008_word.doc.

Equality Act (2010) *Departmental Advice.* Available online at: http://www.education.gov.uk/a0064570/-equality-act-2010.

European Commission (2005) *Special Eurobarometer 224, Wave 63.1*, Brussels. Available online at: http://ec.europa.eu/health/eurobarometers.

European Commission (2009) *Eurobarometer no. 239 – Young People and Science.* Available online at: http://ec.europa.eu/health/eurobarometers.

European Labour Force Survey (2007) Available online at: http://www.esds.ac.uk/government/lfs.

Falk, J. and Dierking, L. (1997) School field trips: assessing their long-term impact. *Curator*, 40: 211–218.

Francis, B., Osgood, J., Dalgety, J. and Archer, L. (2005) *Gender Equality in Work.* A report by the London Metropolitan University, commissioned by the Equal Opportunities Commission. Available online at: www.educationandemployers.org/research/research-reports/young-people/gender-equality.

Future Morph (2011) *Equality and Diversity.* Available online at: http://www.futuremorph.org/wp-content/uploads/2012/03/4.Equality-and-diversity3.pdf

Gallup Organization (2009) *Flash Eurobarometer 239. Young People and Science, Analytical Report.* Available online at: http://ec.europa.eu/public_opinion/flash/fl_239_en.pdf.

Gibson, C. (1911) *The Autobiography of an Electron.* Philadelphia, PA: J.B. Lippincott.

Giffould, J. (2011) *Practical Experiments in School Science Lessons and Science Field Trips – Science and Technology Committee, Parliamentary Business.* Available online at: http://www.publications.parliament.uk/pa/cm201012/cmselect/cmsctech/1060/1060vw03.htm.

Guardian (2013) *The School We'd Like Competition.* Available online at: http://www.guardian.co.uk/teacher-network/2013/jan/21/school-we-d-like-competition-regional-finalists.

Health and Safety Executive (2011a) *School Trips and Outdoor Learning Activities: Tackling the Health and Safety Myths.* Available online at: www.hse.gov.uk/services/education/school-trips.pdf.

Health and Safety Executive (2011b) *Providing and Using Work Equipment Safely: A Brief Guide.* Available online at: www.hse.gov.uk/pubns/indg291.pdf.

Health and Safety Executive (2012a) *Five Steps to Risk Assessment.* Available online at: http://www.hse.gov.uk/risk/fivesteps.htm.

Health and Safety Executive (2012b) *Incident Reporting In Schools (Accidents, Diseases and Dangerous Occurrences).* Available online at: www.hse.gov.uk/pubns/edis1.pdf.

Health and Safety Executive (2013a) *Control of Substances Hazardous to Health, The COSHH Regulations (2002).* Available online at: http://www.hse.gov.uk/coshh/index.htm.

Health and Safety Executive (undated) *Frequently Asked Questions About School Trips.* Available online at: http://www.hse.gov.uk/services/education/faqs.htm.

Helm, A. (2012) Finding funding for science and engineering projects. *Primary Science,* 124: Sep/Oct.

Her Majesty's Stationery Office (2006) *Science and Innovation Investment Framework 2004–2014: Next Steps.* London: HMSO.

Heyden, R. (2012) *A Network Effect Case Study: #organellewars.* Available online at: http://robinheyden.wordpress.com/2012/11/08/a-network-effect-case-study-organellewars.

HM Treasury (2004) *Science and Innovation Investment Framework.* Available online at: http://webarchive.nationalarchives.gov.uk/+/http:/www.hm-treasury.gov.uk/spending_sr04_science.htm.

Holman, J. and Finegold, P. (2010) *STEM Careers Review.* Available online at: http://www.nationalstemcentre.org.uk/res/documents/page/STEM%20CAREERS%20REVIEW%20NOV%202010.pdf.

Home Office (2013) *Disclosure and Barring Service.* Available online at: http://www.homeoffice.gov.uk/agencies-public-bodies/dbs/services.

House of Commons Report (2011a) *Practical Experiments in School Science Lessons and Science Field Trips; Science and Technology Committee.* Ninth report of session 2010–2011, HC 1060-11. London: The Stationery Office.

House of Commons Report (2011b) *Educating the Next Generation of Scientists.* Fifteenth report of session 2010–2011, HC 632. London: The Stationery Office.

Howarth, S. and Scott, L. (2011a) Inspirational ideas for STEM clubs and projects from the Big Bang: UK Young Scientists' and Engineers' Fair, 2011. *School Science Review,* 92(341): 25–35.

Howarth, S. and Scott, L. (2011b) Looking forward to 2012 with your STEM/science club. *School Science Review,* 93(343): 19–24.

Howarth, S. and Scott, L. (2012) The most 'awesome' science fair in the UK. *School Science Review,* 93(345): 14–20.

Howarth, S. and Slingsby, D. (2006) Biology fieldwork in school grounds: a model of good practice in teaching science. *School Science Review,* 87(320): 99–104.

Howarth, S. and Woollhead, A. (2008) Sweet science: practical ideas using sweets and biscuits to teach earth science topics in secondary science. *School Science Review,* 89(328): 31–34.

Hoxbury, C. and Avery, C. (2012) *The Missing 'One-Offs': The Hidden Supply of High-Achieving, Low Income Students.* National Bureau of Economic Research working paper no. 18586. Abstract available online at: http://www.nber.org/papers/w18586.

Hughes, W. (2013a) *Science Beyond the Curriculum.* EiSXtra online, February, 2013. Available online at: http://www.ase.org.uk/documents/science-beyond-the-curriculum.

Hughes, W. (2013b) *Working with Car Firms in Birkenhead.* EiSXtra, ASE on-line member's journal.

Information Commissioner's Office (2013) *The Data Protection Act.* Available online at: http://www.ico.gov.uk/for_organisations/data_protection.aspx.

Information Commissioner's Office (undated) *Education – Taking Photos in Schools.* Available online at: http://www.ico.gov.uk/for_organisations/sector_guides/education.aspx.

Instructables (2013) *How To Make Banana Oxidation Art/How to Tattoo a Banana.* Available online at: http://www.instructables.com/id/How-to-Make-Banana-Oxidation-Art-How-to-Tattoo-a-.

Jenkins, E.W. and Nelson, N. (2005) Important but not for me: students' attitudes towards secondary school science in England. *Research in Science & Technological Education,* 23(1): 41–57.

Jenkins, E.W. and Pell, R.G. (2006) *The Relevance of Science Education Project (ROSE) in England: A Summary of Findings.* Leeds: Centre for Studies in Science and Mathematics Education, University of Leeds.

Joint Council for Qualifications (2012a) *Provisional GCE A level Results (All UK Candidates)*. Available online at: http://www.jcq.org.uk/examination-results/a-levels/a-as-and-aea-results-summer-2012.

Joint Council for Qualifications (2012b) *GCSE and Entry Level Certificate Results Summer 2012*. Available online at: http://www.jcq.org.uk/examination-results/gcses/gcse.

Kangshen, S., Crossley, J.N. and Lun, A.W.C. (eds.) (2000) *The Nine Chapters on the Mathematical Art* (English translation). Oxford: Oxford University Press.

Kisiel, J. (2005) Understanding elementary teacher motivations for science fieldtrips. *Science Education*, 89(6): 936–955.

Kroto, H. (2007) *The Wrecking of British Science*. On-line article, The Guardian, Tuesday 22 May. Available online at: http://www.guardian.co.uk/theguardian.

Lotto, R.B. (2011) *Blackawton Bees*. Available online at: http://www.lottolab.org/articles/blackawtonbees.asp.

Lotto, R.G. and O'Toole, A. (2012) *Science Is for Everyone, Kids Included*. Available online at: http://www.ted.com/talks/beau_lotto_amy_o_toole_science_is_for_everyone_kids_included.html.

McCombs, B. (undated) *Developing Responsible and Autonomous Learners: A Key to Motivating Students: Teacher's Modules*. American Psychological Association. Available online at: http://www.apa.org/education/k12/learners.aspx (accessed February 2013).

McGregor, D. and Precious, W. (2013) *Dramatic Science: Using Drama to Inspire Science Teaching for Ages 5 to 8*. Routledge.

McKinsey and Co. (2007) *How the World's Best Performing School Systems Come Out on Top*. Available online at: http://www.mckinsey.com.

Mitchell, M. (1993) Situational interest: its multifaceted structure in the secondary school mathematics classroom. *Journal of Educational Psychology*, 85(3): 424–436.

Mitchell, S., Foulger, T.S., Wetzel, K. and Rathkey, C. (2009) The negotiated project approach: project-based learning without leaving the standards behind. *Early Childhood Education Journal*, 36(4): 339–346.

Munn, M. (ed.) (2011) *Unlocking Potential: Perspectives on Women in Science, Engineering and Technology*. Available online at: http://www.smith-institute.org.uk/file/Women%20in%20SET.pdf.

Museum Network (2008–2009) *The Power of the Object: What Effect Do 'Real' Objects Have on Pupils' Learning?* Available online at: http://www.museumnetworkuk.org/latest-news.

Museum of Science, Boston (2013) *Putting the 'M' in STEM*. Available online at: http://www.mos.org/collaborations/putting-the-m-in-stem.

National Action Council for Minorities in Engineering (2012) *Critical Issues in Engineering Education Policy*, vol. 2. no. 1. Available online at: http://www.nacme.org/NACME_D.aspx?pageid=190.

National Centre for Excellence in the Teaching of Mathematics (2013) *Learning Maths Outside the Classroom*. Available online at: www.ncetm.org.uk/resources/9309.

National Council of Teachers of English (2013) *NCTE Framework for 21st Century Curriculum and Assessment*. Available online at: http://www.ncte.org/library/NCTEFiles/Resources/Positions/Framework_21stCent_Curr_Assessment.pdf.

National Curriculum (2008) Available online at: http://teachfind.com/qcda/programme-study-science-key-stage-4-subjects-key-stages-3-4-national-curriculum.

National Foundation for Educational Research (2011) *The STEM Cohesion Programme: Final Report*. Research report DFE-RR147. Available online at: https://www.education.gov.uk/publications/standard/publicationDetail/Page1/DFE-RR147.

National Society for the Prevention of Cruelty to Children (2012) *Child Protection Legislation in the UK Factsheet*. Available online at: http://www.nspcc.org.uk/Inform/research/questions/child_protection_legislation_in_the_uk_wda48946.html.

National STEM Centre (2000–2009) *Enhancement, Enrichment and Partnerships.* Available online at: http://www.nationalstemcentre.org.uk/elibrary/collection/278/enhancement-enrichment-and-partnerships.

National STEM Centre (March 2013a) Available online at: http://www.nationalstemcentre.org.uk/stem-in-context/what-is-stem.

National STEM Centre (2013b) *On-line STEM Planning Tools.* Available online at: http://www.nationalstemcentre.org.uk/stem-in-context/stem-planning-tools.

National Strategies (2008) *Interactive Practicals Science Study Guide.* Department for Children, Schools and Families. Available online at: http://nationalstrategies.standards.dcsf.gov.uk/node/284937.

Natural History Museum (2004) *Walking with Woodlice Project.* Available online at: http://www.nhm.ac.uk/woodlice.

Needham, R. (2013) Twitter, my best CPD ever! *Primary Science,* 127 (March/April): 8–9.

Newnham, D. (2008) *Passion for the Past.* First published in TES Newspaper 14 January 2000, updated 11 May 2008. Available online at: http://www.tes.co.uk/article.aspx?storycode=329895.

Ofsted (2008) *Schools and Sustainability.* Available online at: http://www.ofsted.gov.uk/resources/schools-and-sustainability.

Ofsted (2010) *Learning Outside the Classroom: How Far Should You Go?* Available online at: https://www.education.gov.uk/publications/standard/publicationDetail/Page1/HMI-070219.

Ofsted (2011a) *Successful Science: An Evaluation of Science Education in England 2007–2010.* Available online at: www.ofsted.gov.uk/resources/successful-science.

Ofsted (2011b) *Making Technological Challenges?* Design and technology in schools, 2007–10, March 2011. Report no 100121. Available online at: http://www.ofsted.gov.uk/resources/meeting-technological-challenges.

Ofsted (2011c) *Girls' Career Aspirations.* Available online at: www.ofsted.gov.uk/resources/girls-career-aspirations.

Ofsted (2012a) *Guidance to Inspecting E-Safety (and more).* Available online at: http://www.ofsted.gov.uk/resources/briefings-and-information-for-use-during-inspections-of-maintained-schools-and-academies-january-201.

Ofsted (2012b) *Mathematics: Made to Measure.* Available online at: http://www.ofsted.gov.uk/resources/mathematics-made-measure.

Osborne, J. and Collins, S. (2000) Pupils' and parents' views of school science curriculum. *School Science Review,* 82(298): 23–31.

Osborne, J. and Dillon, J. (2008) *Science Education in Europe: Critical Reflections.* Available online at: www.nuffieldfoundation.org/sites/default/files/Sci_Ed_in_Europe_Report_Final.pdf.

Osterrieder, A. (2012) *The Organelle Presidential Campaign.* Available online at: http://www.plantcellbiology.com/2012/10/the-organelle-presidential-campaign-2012.

Paczuska, A. and Steedman, S. (2012) *After-School Clubs.* Ingenia online. Available online at: http://www.ingenia.org.uk/ingenia/articles.aspx?Index=761.

Passy, R., Morris, M. and Reed, F. (2010) *Impact of School Gardening on Learning: Final Report Submitted to the Royal Horticultural Society.* Slough: National Foundation for Educational Research (NFER).

Pearson Education (2012) *Edexcel's STEM Leadership Qualification.* Available online at: http://www.edexcel.com/quals/workskills/stem/Pages/default.aspx.

Pintrich, P.R. (2003) A motivational science perspective on the role of student motivation in learning and teaching contexts. *Journal of Educational Psychology,* 95(4): 667–686.

Pitt, J. (2009) Blurring the boundaries – STEM education and education for sustainable development. *Design and Technology Education: An International Journal,* 14(1): 37–48.

Price-Mitchell, M. (2011) *Mistakes Improve Children's Learning*. Available online at: http://www.psychologytoday.com/blog/the-moment-youth/201109/mistakes-improve-childrens-learning.

Programme for International Student Assessment in Focus (2012) *Are Students More Engaged When Schools Offer Extracurricular Activities?* PISA in Focus 18. Available online at: http://www.oecd.org/pisa/pisainfocus/#d.en.199059.

Public Policy Exchange Symposium (2013) *Strengthening the Roles of Careers Guidance in Schools and Colleges*. Available online at: http://publicpolicyexchange.co.uk/docs/DA22-PPE_flyer.pdf.

Ramirez, R. (2013) *Save Our Science: How to Inspire a New Generation of Scientists*. Kindle Single, TED Books.

Rasekoala, E. (2001) *African-Caribbean Representation in Science & Technology (ACRISAT)*. London, UK: National Endowment for Science, Technology and the Arts.

RBS Group (2012) *Women in Enterprise: A Different Perspective*. Available online at: http://www.inspiringenterprise.rbs.com/sites/default/files/Women_in_Enterprise.pdf.

Reiss, M. and Tunnicliffe, S.D. (2011) Dioramas as depictions of reality and opportunities for learning in biology. *Curator*, 54: 447–459.

Roberts, G. (2002) *SET for Success*, review. Available online at: http://www.nationalstemcentre.org.uk/stem-programme/stem-background.

Rothstein, D. and Santana, L. (2011) *Make Just One Change: Teach Students to Ask Their Own Questions*. Harvard, MA: Harvard Education Press.

Royal Academy of Engineering (2011) *Notes for STEM Clubs and STEM Ambassador Resources, Engineering Engagement Project*. Available online at: http://www.raeng.org.uk/education/eenp/engineering_resources/pdf/Hazard_Sheet.pdf.

Royal Society (2006) *Taking a Leading Role – Scientists Survey*. Available online at: http://royalsociety.org/uploadedFiles/Royal_Society_Content/Supporting_scientists/Equality_and_Diversity/Scientists_survey.pdf.

Royal Society of Chemistry (2007) *Surely That's Banned?* Available online at: http://www.rsc.org/ScienceAndTechnology/Policy/Bulletins/Issue5/SurelyThatsBanned.asp.

Sainsbury, D. (2007) *The Race to the Top: A Review of Government's Science and Innovation Policies*. London: HMSO.

Salmi, H. (2003) Science centres as learning laboratories: experiences of Heureka, the Finnish Science Centre. *International Journal of Technology Management*, 25: 460–476.

Saul, W., Kohnen, A., Newman, A. and Pearce, L. (2011) *Front-Page Science: Engaging Teens in Science Literacy*. Arlington, VA: National Science Teachers Association, NSTA Press.

Science, Technology, Engineering and Mathematics (STEM) programme report (2006) Available online at: http://www.nationalstemcentre.org.uk/stem-programme/stem-background.

Scott, L. and Howarth, S. (2011) New academic year, new science/STEM club? *School Science Review*, 93(342): 31–36.

Scott, L. and Howarth, S. (2012a) Marketing and extending your STEM club. *School Science Review*, 94(347): 19–22.

Scott, L. and Howarth, S. (2012b) Creative gardening as a STEM club activity. *School Science Review*, 93(344): 18–22.

Scottish Schools Education Research Centre (2013) *Science Festivals*. Available online at: http://www.science3-18.org/sserc/index.php?option=com_content&view=article&id=2107:science-festivals&catid=408:events-external&Itemid=715.

Settlage, J. and Southerland, S. (2012) *Teaching Science to Every Child: Using Culture as a Starting Point*. New York: Routledge.

Simmons, A. and Page, M. (2010) Motivating students through power and choice. *English Journal*, 100(1): 65–69.

Sjøberg, S. (2004) *Attitudes and Interests in Science and Technology*. Paper presented to a conference on Increasing Human Resources for Science and Technology in Europe. Brussels: European Commission.

Sjøberg, S. and Schreiner, C. (2010) *ROSE, Relevance of Science Education, Project*. Overview and key findings. Available online at: nor-Sjoberg-Schreiner-overview-2010-1.pdf.

Smith, A. (2004) *Making Mathematics Count, Inquiry*. Available online at: dera.ioe.ac.uk/4873/1/MathsInquiryFinalReport.pdf.

Smith, F. (2013) We're all going to the zoo tomorrow. *Primary Science*, 126: 23–26.

Spalding, V. (2012) *We are Researchers!* ASE Research Seminar Series. Liverpool: AQA's Centre for Education Research and Policy, University of Liverpool.

Springate, I., Harland, J., Lord, P. and Wilkin, A. (2008) *The Factors Affecting A-Level and Undergraduate Subject Choice in Physics and Chemistry by Ethnic Group*. NFER research report. Available online at: http://www.nfer.ac.uk/nfer/publications/AUC01/AUC01_home.cfm?publicationID=95&title=factors%20affecting%20A-level%20and%20undergraduate%20subject%20choice%20in%20physics%20and%20chemistry%20by%20ethnic%20group.

Springate, I., Harland, J., Lord, P. and Straw, S. (2009) *Evaluation of the 2008–09 DCSF-funded Specialist Schools and Academies Trust STEM Pathfinder Programme: Executive Summary*. Slough: NFER.

STEM Clubs (2013) *What Is a STEM Club?* Available online at: http://www.stemclubs.net/about.

STEMNET (2013) *STEM Clubs Guide*. Available online at: http://www.stemclubs.net/guides/498/activity_ideas.

Straw, S., Hart, R. and Harland, J. (2011) *An Evaluation of the Impact of STEMNET's Services on Pupils and Teacher*. Slough: NFER.

Success in Schools (2013) *Safeguarding Changes – January 2013*. Available online at: http://www.successinschools.co.uk/safeguarding-changes-january-2013.

Sundem, G. (undated) *How to Defeat a Dragon with Math*, TED-Ed video. Available online at: http://ed.ted.com/lessons/how-to-defeat-a-dragon-with-math-garth-sundem.

Sutton Trust (2011) *Education Endowment Foundation Teaching and Learning Toolkit*. Available online at: http://educationendowmentfoundation.org.uk/toolkit.

The Engineer (2011) School design and technology lessons are 'out of date'. Available online at: http://www.theengineer.co.uk/school-design-and-technology-lessons-are-out-of-date/1008017.article#ixzz2L4FCkfVs.

Thomas Hardye School (2010) *Jurassic Poetry and Music Booklet*. Available online at: http://www.thomas-hardye.dorset.sch.uk/pages/news/news_2010/03_10/science_week.php.

Tomsett, J. (2012) *This Much I Know About ... Teaching Disengaged 15 Year Old Boys*, posted 6 October. Available online at: http://johntomsett.wordpress.com/2012/10/06/this-much-i-know-aboutteaching-disengaged-15-year-old-boys.

Tosh, M. and Short, D. (2009) Science, technology, engineering and maths (STEM) clubs: starting out. *School Science Review*, 91(334): 51–56.

Trends in International Mathematics and Science Study (TIMSS) Available online at: http://timss.bc.edu.

Tyson, W., Lee, R., Borman, K. and Hanson, M. (2007) Science, technology, engineering, and mathematics (STEM) pathways: high school science and math coursework and postsecondary degree attainment. *Journal of Education for Students Placed at Risk (JESPAR)*, 12(3): 243–270.

Tytler, R., Osborne, J., Williams, G., Tytler, K. and Cripps Clark, J. (2008) *Opening Up Pathways: Engagement in STEM Across the Primary–Secondary School Transition*. Canberra, ACT: Australian Department of Education, Employment and Workplace Relations.

UK Commission for Employment and Skills (2011) *The Supply of and Demand for High-level STEM Skills*. Briefing paper. Available online at: www.ukces.org.uk.

UK Environmental Law Association (2011) *Waste Electrical and Electronic Equipment (WEEE)*. Available online at: http://www.environmentlaw.org.uk/rte.asp?id=245.

UKRC (2010) *Women and Men in Science, Engineering and Technology: The UK Statistics Guide*. Available online at: http://www.napier.ac.uk/research/centresandprojects/src/Documents/final-sept-15th-15-42-ukrc-statistics-guide-2010.pdf.

United Nations Development Programme (2013) *Human Development Report*. Available online at: http://hdr.undp.org/en/media/HDR%202013%20technical%20notes%20EN.pdf.

University of Bristol, Graduate School of Education. (2012) *The Bristol Guide. Professionals in Schools: Roles and Responsibilities*. Updated yearly. Available online at: www.bristol.ac.uk/education/expertiseandresources/bristolguide.

University of Warwick (2009) *Lengthening Ladders, Shortening Snakes: Embedding STEM Careers Awareness in Secondary Schools*. Available online at: http://www.nationalstemcentre.org.uk/res/documents/page/lengthening_ladders_shortening_snakes.pdf.

US Congress Joint Economic Committee (2012) *STEM Education: Preparing for the Jobs of the Future*. Available online at: http://www.jec.senate.gov/public/index.cfm?a=Files.Serve&File_id=6aaa7e1f-9586-47be-82e7-326f47658320.

US Department of Commerce, Economics and Statistics Administration (2011a) *STEM: Good Jobs Now and for the Future*. ESA issue brief #03. Available online at: esa.doc.gov/sites/default/files/reports/documents/stemfinalyjuly14_1.pdf.

US Department of Commerce, Economics and Statistics Administration (2011b) *Women in STEM: A Gender Gap to Innovation*. Available online at: http://www.esa.gov/sites/default/files/reports/documents/womeninstemagaptoinnovation8311.pdf.

Wadley, J (2012) *My Fair Physicist? Feminine Math, Science Role Models Do Not Motivate Girls*. Available online at: http://www.ns.umich.edu/new/releases/20355-my-fair-physicist-feminine-math-science-role-models-do-not-motivate-girls (accessed 11 January 2013).

Walker, I. and Zhu, Y. (2011) Differences by degree: evidence of the net financial rates of return to undergraduate study for England and Wales. *Economics of Education Review*, 30(6): 1177–1186.

Weeks, S. (2012) Polar science is cool. *Primary Science*, 125(November): 27–30.

Wellcome Trust (2010) *Subject Choice in STEM: Factors Influencing Young People (aged 14–19) in Education. A Systematic Review of the UK Literature*. Available online at: http://www.wellcome.ac.uk/stellent/groups/corporatesite/@msh_publishing_group/documents/web_document/wtx063082.pdf

Wellcome Trust (2012) *Review of Informal Science Learning, Science Beyond the Classroom*. GHK Consulting and Stanford and Oregon Universities; summary of the two reports. Available online at: http://www.wellcome.ac.uk/About-us/Publications/Reports/Education/index.htm.

Williams, J. (2011). STEM education: proceed with caution. *Design and Technology Education*, 16(1): 26–35.

Wilson, H. and Mant, J. (2011) What makes and exemplary teacher of science? The pupils' perspective. *School Science Review*, 93(342): 121–125.

Zollman, A. (2012) Learning for STEM literacy: STEM literacy for learning. *School Science and Mathematics*, 112(1): 12–19.

Index